Beyond Texting

The Fine Art of
Face-To-Face Communication
For Teenagers

Also By Debra Fine

The Fine Art of Small Talk

The Fine Art of the Big Talk

BEYOND TEXTING

The Fine Art of

Face-To-Face Communication For Teenagers

Debra Fine

CANON PUBLISHERS

Library of Congress Cataloging-in-Publication Data: 2013941019

Fine, Debra
Beyond texting: the fine art of face-to-face-communication for teenagers / Debra Fine
    p. cm.
   ISBN: 0988969602
    1. Communication 2. Oral communication 3. Young Adult 4. Self -Help
   ISBN: – 13 978-0988969605

FIRST EDITION

Dedicated with love to the two who taught me the most:
Jared Fine Holst and Sarah Fine Holst and for Steve Tilliss who
makes my teenage years a small price to pay.

Contents

Beyond Texting: The Fine Art of
Face-To-Face Communication For Teenagers

CONTENTS

ACKNOWLEDGEMENTS

Huge thanks to the dedication and passion of Rachel Salter who brought her great writing skills to this project. Not only is she far closer in age to a teen, but her big heart better hears the beat of a teen's drum. Her insight and contribution were the exact balance for whatever communication skills I offered. Patti Thorn, editor to the stars (and all of us that hope to be), always found the time to lend her expertise to this project. Despite a myriad of challenges she was with me for the entire journey. What author doesn't need a few magic tricks along with a dose of chicken soup wisdom? It is always there for me from Stacey Miller, my queen of PR who along with the man of my dreams Steve Tilliss sings a consistent chorus of "I'm a Believer" whenever I mention a project. Lastly, thank you to all those who have reached out to me asking for a book for teens. I appreciate the kick in the butt.

INTRODUCTION

When I look back on my years as a teenager, I recall how uncomfortable I felt in so many situations. I trembled at the thought of having to stand in front of a class and give a ten-minute oral presentation. I retreated like a turtle into my shell anytime a boy tried to talk to me. I was terrified to go to parties and events where I didn't know many people, fearing I'd end up standing in a corner alone or desperately trying to think of clever ways to strike up a conversation with a stranger—with little success. I wasn't necessarily shy; I just didn't have the right communication skills to give me the confidence I needed.

I wouldn't be at all surprised if you feel the same way. It almost seems as if communication has a secret code—a complicated formula that isn't written anywhere, but one everyone else seems to understand. If only you, too, could crack the code, success would be automatic.

During this critical time in your life, you're just beginning to learn what to say and how to say it, as well as what not to say. Every word or action seems like it will shape your entire life. While this is not completely true, every word or action *can* lead to a conversation, which can lead to relationships that become the foundation of your life. One of the most valuable skills you can learn is the art of interacting and communicating with all kinds of people, from classmates and friends to parents, coaches and teachers.

Today, obtaining that skill is more challenging than ever. While the basic communication fears you have are probably similar to the ones teens had decades ago, technology has added many new twists. Facebook, Twitter, Instant Messenger and text messaging now play a huge role in how you communicate with your friends, family and others. These are great advancements in that they allow you to exchange information immediately and give you more choices in how to interact with others. But the more you rely on these devices, the more they can interfere with your comfort level when you communicate in person.

Think about it: You're signed up for phone plans that give you unlimited text messages but only 200 "talk" minutes. You send birthday wishes, congratulations and thank you notes by tapping keys on a machine more often than relaying the message in person. You learn to display emoticons, but showing your emotions is another thing altogether. You can seamlessly connect to the web, but do you feel comfortable connecting with the person sitting next to you in class?

Digital communication is not going away; if anything, it's bound to become more prevalent. In fact, new technologies for communicating are appearing all the time. So we all need to learn how to maintain the social skills we rely on to be active participants in the real world.

That's where this book comes in. In *Beyond Texting*, I aim to give you the tools you need to successfully communicate with others in order to develop lasting, productive and meaningful relationships. On these pages, I'll teach you how to start a conversation, keep a conversation going and leave a positive impression. I'll teach you how to approach authority figures confidently and say "no" to peers, even when it seems impossible. And I'll show you how to balance technology-based and real-life interactions so you can set yourself up for future success.

I'm not saying it will be easy. To improve your skills, you will have to take some risks. You may have to force yourself to talk to strangers you'd rather avoid at a meeting or party, or apply for a job even though you're terrified of interviewing. You may have to say "no" to someone who's offering you a ride home after drinking, or convey your disappointment to a friend who's behaving badly. These are difficult interactions, but I promise if you can challenge yourself in these ways, you'll soon develop positive practices that will be essential later in life as you start a career, establish important friendships and search for romantic relationships.

I know it can work for you, because it worked for me. After years of practice, I'm no longer hesitant to strike up a conversation with a stranger at a party or to speak in front of a large group of people. In fact, I do this frequently for my work as a keynote speaker, talking to as many as 2,000 audience members at a time! Still, I often regret that it took me so long to develop these strong communication skills.

If you're reading this book, you're clearly determined not to make that same mistake. I applaud your desire to improve yourself and will show you how to do so, step by step.

Now let's get started!

SECTION I

Conquering The Conversational Basics

CHAPTER I

BOOTING UP:
*Why mastering conversational skills now will
pay off later in life*

Life is defined by the relationships one builds through
various experiences, and it is effective communication that
allows these relationships to develop and flourish. In your teen
years, it may not seem important to refine your conversational
skills (most teens say what they want and don't think much
about the long-term impact), but whether you realize it or
not, your everyday interactions are preparing you for real-
world interactions that will influence your employment,
relationships and even success in society in years to come.

Whether you're in middle school, high school or college,
it's important to use every opportunity possible to establish
a strong foundation of conversational skills. When it comes
time to have a serious romantic relationship, apply for a job

or make friends without the assistance of a structured setting, your ability to converse effectively will be your biggest asset.

Here are three main relationships to consider as they are now and how they'll translate later in life:

Now: Teacher
Later: Boss

One way to think about your teacher is as your boss, the person to whom you report. She is in charge of making sure you're as productive as possible and that you're applying yourself to the best of your abilities. If you learn to work well with your teachers now, you will be in a better position to know how to deal with your bosses later in life.

Take Maggie, for example. She's graduating from college in three months and is looking for employment. Throughout high school and college, Maggie emphasized open communication between herself and her instructors. She spoke up in class, asked questions and made it a point to have teachers know her name and her studious work habits. When it came time to turn in a big paper, she would ask for feedback on details she wasn't sure about, and when she had an assignment that interested her, she would run her ideas by the teacher well ahead of the due date.

In a job market that's challenging and competitive, one in which employers have their pick of many qualified candidates, Maggie stands out. What sets her apart from others with similar education and experience? She's able to present herself maturely and with confidence, a skill she spent her teen years thoughtfully perfecting. Not only will she success-fully land a job, she'll successfully interact with her superiors and colleagues.

Now: School peers and friends
Later: Work relationships

Today, the majority of your friendships most likely stem from school and extra-curricular activities. These controlled environments allow friendships to flourish. However, later in life, making friends can be a bit more challenging. In the workplace, for example, you'll come across a greater diversity of people, many of whom have very different backgrounds than your own. That's why developing skills to build and maintain friendships early on is so important. If you learn communication styles that attract friends now you'll be more likely to have the skills you need to build relationships in the workplace, and good professional relationships will make your work life more easy, satisfying and rewarding.

Now: High school sweetheart
Later: Long-term partner

You often hear that the key to a successful marriage is communication. So isn't it best to enter into a serious relationship with those skills already in place? While chemistry and physical attraction can be the hook that draws you to another, it's your verbal and listening skills—your ability to understand the other person—that will ultimately keep you tuned in and connected. When you and your partner can discuss your problems and fears and dreams and plans in an honest, caring way, you set yourself up for long-term understanding and support.

Here's an exercise to gauge how well you communicate with your boyfriend or girlfriend. Answer "yes" or "no" to the following questions:

1. Do you know where your girlfriend wants to be in terms of career, relationship, and geographic location in five years?
2. Have you talked to your boyfriend about his core values and what is fundamentally important to him?
3. Do you know what makes your relationship successful?
4. Do you know what you need to work on in your relationship?
5. Are you aware of your girlfriend's fears, insecurities and weaknesses?
6. Do you know how your boyfriend defines happiness?
7. Have you discussed career goals and ambitions with your girlfriend?
8. Do you know how your boyfriend would respond to failure or rejection?
9. Would you describe your relationship as one in which you and your girlfriend are often on the same page?
10. Do you trust your boyfriend?

If you answered "yes" to these questions, then you're on your way to establishing valuable communication skills that will help you build a satisfying long-term relationship. If you answered "no" to these questions, then use them as prompts to dig deeper into your relationship and learn about your partner. By doing this, you'll learn better communication skills along the way.

Whether this is the person you'll spend the rest of your life with or not, it's critical to develop communication intimacy in order to be the best possible contributor to a partnership—now and in the future.

POKE → The real world is full of challenges, but if you're adequately equipped to communicate and able to understand the fundamentals in which relationships thrive, you'll have a greater chance for success.

CHAPTER 2

LOGGING ON:
Opening yourself up to others comes first

The first step to becoming a good communicator is becoming a good conversationalist. A good conversationalist makes others feel comfortable while taking ownership of the conversation.

The key element to becoming a first-rate conversationalist is to be open to others. It's hard to risk rejection, which can cause fearfulness, even in adults. No doubt you've often let that terror stop you from approaching others. To make matters even more difficult, from birth you've most likely been taught several notions that only hinder your desire to take a risk and start a conversation. Do these lines sound familiar?

- **"Good things come to those who wait."**
- **"Only speak when spoken to."**

- **"Don't talk to strangers."**

When it comes to the art of conversation, I urge you to throw all these ideas far out the window. It's one thing to mind your manners, it's another to let these silly childhood concepts prevent you from meeting people.

Let's examine each saying and establish a better way to interact with others.

"Good things come to those who wait."

This is rarely true. Actually, good things come to those who go get them!

In social situations, waiting for others to initiate a conversation is likely to leave you sitting in a corner by yourself. If you wait around at a party for someone to come talk to you, you may be waiting all night. If you wait until the girl you like messages you on Facebook, you may never get the chance to talk to her in person.

Don't be afraid to make the first move. Instead of counting on that girl to send you a message, strike up a conversation at school. She'll respect your confidence and be more likely to want a real connection with you. Look for the person at the party standing alone or not already engaged in a conversation. I guarantee this person will be just as relieved as you are to talk to someone. Take the plunge and approach them. The next time you join a group for lunch, consider inviting someone new to join as well. It's worth the risk. And in truth, the chance of actual rejection is pretty remote; it exists more in your mind than in reality. Besides, without taking the risk, you'll never reap the wonderful rewards that meeting new people can bring to you.

"Don't speak until spoken to."

Sure, this rule may have made sense when your parents were having a dinner party and you were six years old. But now that you've grown up, it's your responsibility to speak up. You can't rely on someone else to initiate contact —and you shouldn't. Silence won't get you very far.

Think about the most successful students, the most well-rounded classmates and involved peers. Are they keeping their mouths shut? I doubt it. They're friendly and engaged, offering their opinions to others, speaking up in class, volunteering for leadership positions in clubs and extracurricular activities. Keeping silent can be more detrimental than you think; shy and reserved people often come off as arrogant and pretentious. If you're seen in this light, it can badly damage your social image.

Don't be perceived this way; start talking and stop the silence. You might target the Student Council president after a meeting and offer those ideas you didn't get a chance to convey during the meeting, or you might simply smile and say hello to a student you sit next to in class or band. If you think you know the answer to a question or have a comment to share in class, don't wait until the teacher calls on you. Raising your hand and offering your ideas will make you seem friendly and confident to everyone in the room, even if you get the answer wrong.

When you speak up you'll feel empowered as you share your opinions and gain the experience of talking to different individuals.

"Don't talk to strangers."

If we didn't talk to strangers, we would live in a very quiet world. It's an important rule to follow when you're five, but as a teenager you have to begin pushing the boundaries of your comfort level. Talking to strangers is like visiting a foreign country: It's somewhat exotic and you're likely to experience a combination of nervousness and excitement while exploring unfamiliar territory. But you're ultimately going to walk away feeling invigorated from the novel encounter.

Strangers have the potential to open doorways to unforeseen friendships and opportunities. My friend Steve is a master of striking up small talk with strangers. While traveling in Italy with his wife and teenagers, he began talking with a local woman about the magazine she was reading. The encounter spurred the woman to invite Steve and his family to her house on the Venice Grand Canal, where they sat on a magnificent balcony and watched the gondolas pass by. While his teens were initially embarrassed about his gregarious approach, in the end they were impressed by the woman's home and the authentic experience their father's simple gesture ultimately added to their Italian travels.

Begin thinking of strangers you encounter in safe environments as people who can bring new dimensions to your life, not persons to be feared. To eliminate any safety concerns, limit your efforts to reach out to selected strangers in environments you trust, say, new people at church/synagogue events, a student at your lunch table you've never talked to, or a fellow attendee at an SAT prep class.

I know this will be uncomfortable at first. It's much easier to ask an acquaintance or a familiar face to be your "friend" on a social networking site than to introduce yourself in person. But it's important not to let computers do all the interacting for you, even if that seems easy and effortless. The key to creating a strong social community is to personally interact with others, an approach I guarantee will be more lasting and intimate than spending all your time and attention building your online social network.

Well, how did you do? If you answered ten or more of the above with a "yes," then you're a master at meeting new people. You're proficient in making yourself available to new

---

How are you at meeting new people?

Please answer "yes" or "no" to the following questions:

1. I have joined or participated in at least one club, sport or group activity this year. ____ Yes ____ No
2. I have raised my hand in class within the last week. ___ Yes ___ No
3. I have friends who participate in at least one school or non-school extracurricular activity. ____ Yes ____ No
4. I have friends outside of school. ____ Yes ____ No

---

5. I go to at least one extracurricular activity a month where I can meet new people. ____ Yes ____ No

6. When someone asks me "what's new?" I often talk about something exciting in my life instead of saying "not much." ____Yes ____No

7. I vary the groups of friends I hang out with during lunch, after school and during summer break. ____Yes ____No

8. At school, extracurricular activities, camp, parties, etc., I often introduce myself to people I don't know and come away knowing the names of at least three new people. ____Yes ____No

9. I spend more time interacting with people in person than I do on social networking sites. ____Yes ____No

10. If someone is friendly toward me, it's easy to be friendly back. ____ Yes ____ No

11. I'm conscious of "taking turns" in most conversations so I can find out about others and help them get to know me. ____ Yes ____ No

12. I've attended school events such as charity fundraisers, football games, dances, cross-country meets, plays or pep rallies in the past six months. ____Yes ____No

13. In the past, I've approached someone new because I thought they seemed interesting or was romantically attracted to them. ____Yes ____No

relationships and interacting with people. Answering "yes" to at least seven of the questions means you're on your way to becoming a master. You're generally comfortable meeting new people but may be shy and uncertain in new and unfamiliar situations. If you answered "yes" to fewer than seven of the questions, you need a little help learning skills that will make you a social superstar. If you're eager and open to learning such skills, this will be simple and fun.

POKE → You have to take communication risks to reap the relationship rewards.

Exercise:

In order to become more comfortable meeting new people, try to make yourself do three things you wouldn't normally do. You could try out for the school play, introduce yourself to someone you don't know at your dance studio, stay after class to talk to your teacher, start a conversation with one of your parent's friends, go to a job interview even if you don't want the job, or join the debate club. These are all great ways to become more comfortable and familiar with speaking and initiating productive conversations. Just as you train for a sport to become a better player, rehearse your lines to ensure a stellar performance or hit the books hard to master a subject, you must practice communication—especially the hard parts such as approaching new people and starting conversations.

CHAPTER 3

ENTERING THE CHATROOM:
How to approach others and break the ice

So now you know how important starting a conversation is to building relationships and interacting with others. But once you've committed to practicing your conversational skills, how can you make the challenge easier? This next chapter is designed to help you put theory into practice, with simple advice on how to present yourself confidently, break the ice and leave a lasting and positive impression. Follow these basic tips and you'll be communicating like a pro in no time.

1) Exude positive energy and establish a presence.

In unfamiliar situations, it's completely normal to feel nervous and overwhelmed. When faced with these moments, take a deep breath and try to appear relaxed and at ease. Practice making eye contact with everyone while you walk down the hall at school, or smile at strangers you see at the mall. Think about situations when you felt very confident and try to feel that same way again. You may have to fake confidence and comfort at first, and that's completely allowed at this stage. These small steps will help you feel more secure and get you ready for further advancements.

Keep in mind that this technique does not mean you can fake who you are deep inside; it only means you can fake an attitude in order to exude confidence. It means having a firm handshake, making eye contact, standing tall, speaking clearly and loudly and smiling or laughing. Notice how people are automatically drawn to those who are laughing and having a good time? It's not coincidence. Most want to be part of positive experiences. In the same way, however, people are less likely to approach those who appear closed off as they look down at the floor and sulk.

Exuding confidence also means speaking in a way that says, "I know what I'm talking about." You accomplish this by using your best vocabulary and not rushing your words or speaking in a monotone. You want to appear upbeat, engaged, energetic and lively. Take some time in front of the mirror viewing what this looks like for you. Become aware of the placement of your hands and the smile on your face. Do this often until you find a comfort zone in the way you hold yourself. Soon you'll be carrying on confidently and not even realize it because it will have become a habit. The fake act will fade away and you'll be genuinely poised.

2) Break the ice.

Imagine a thick piece of ice, its solid mass nearly impossible to crack. Starting a conversation can often feel the same way—impermeable—as it often requires that you not only engage someone but chip away at their defenses to get to a point where the ice melts and conversation flows. Initiating such a conversation can be scary, but it's not as difficult as you may think. You just have to be equipped with cool conversation ideas.

Here are a few suggestions of conversation starters:

- "How'd you do on the test? I got a B+."
- "What do you think about the new soccer coach?"

- "It seems like you're really good at biology. Do you think we could study for the next exam together?"
- "I love your shoes. Where did you get them?"
- "Nice Broncos jersey. Are you going to watch the game this weekend?"
- "What are your plans this summer? Are you taking any trips?"
- "Nice Kings of Leon T-shirt. Did you hear they're playing in town next month?"
- "I think I was sitting right behind you at the assembly today. What did you think about it?"
- "Didn't I see you at the Intra-Fraternity Council event? What do you like about being in a sorority?"
- "Where do you like to study?"
- "What'd you do over break?"
- "Do you like your job?"
- "I love this website—have you ever seen it?"
- "Did you hear about (a recent news item)?"
- "What do you usually do after school?"

You'll notice that most of these conversation starters have a lot in common. We'll talk more in the next chapter about asking questions, using compliments and taking cues from your immediate surroundings.

Many people search for the "perfect" icebreaker, something that's a guaranteed conversation starter. But there's no way to guarantee that any icebreaker will be "perfect," because we have no idea how someone will respond to what we say. Instead of searching for perfection, just be the first to say "Hello" and don't worry about being judged or rejected. Sure, it happens. Some people make the decision of whether or not they will respond to you based on superficial reasons. Perhaps they're not interested because they've decided you're too tall, too short or wearing the "wrong" clothes. Perhaps they're prejudiced against jocks or math geeks. People can be that shallow. But often we're rejected because of something completely out of our control, like when something has happened at home and the person we're approaching is distracted, or maybe that person failed a test and is upset.

In reality, most of us decide whether or not we'll talk to someone based not on what they say but rather on whether or not we have the time, the interest, or are in the right mood. So stop the treasure hunt for the "perfect" icebreaker. Simply take the risk to say "Hello" and use one of the suggestions above, or come up with engaging, genuine questions of your own.

3) Introduce or re-introduce yourself to the person, even if you think they know who you are.

Check out the following scenario:

Evan and James sit next to each other in geometry class, but they don't ever talk to each other. After class, Evan approaches James to get to know him a little better.

Evan: "Hey, how'd you do on the quiz?"
James: "I got a B. How about you?"

Evan: "I got a C, but was hoping I did better. My name's...."

James: "Evan, right? I'm James. You go to the rec center, right? I think I've seen you there on the weekends."

Evan: "Yeah, I go there with my family. If you're there next weekend, maybe we could shoot some hoops."

James: "That sounds cool. See you tomorrow in class."

Here, Evan broke the ice and James recalled who Evan was and the conversation move forward from there. James was then able to initiate a plan to hang out in a setting where they could learn more about one another and potentially build a friendship.

Romantic interests

Possibly one of the most difficult situations you'll face will be introducing yourself to a potential love interest. Having a crush at a distance is one thing, but actually approaching that person is beyond intimidating. The best way to get your crush to notice you without being completely awkward or allowing yourself to be too vulnerable is to follow the advice in this chapter: Be confident, break the ice and introduce or re-introduce yourself.

Take the following example involving Mia, a junior, who has had a crush on fellow student Javier since the start of the school year. She finally approaches him, though they've never talked before.

Mia: (Standing up straight and speaking clearly) "Hi. I saw you carrying around a Cory Doctorow book earlier—he's really great."

Javier: "Yeah, I'm really enjoying that book."

Mia: (With a smile) "I'm Mia, by the way—I don't think we've officially met."

Javier: "Hi, Mia—I'm Javier."

Mia: "Have you read his book <u>Little Brother</u> yet?"

By confidently carrying herself and smiling at Javier, Mia has made him instantly comfortable around her. She brought up something she knew they could talk about, breaking right through the thick shelf of ice that had been between them for months. Then she introduced herself so Javier will remember the name of the girl with whom he had this interesting conversation.

Here's another scenario:

John is in college. Every morning on his way to class he grabs a cup of coffee from the campus coffee shop. And almost every morning he sees the same woman there. He thinks she's attractive and they've exchanged a few smiles, but he's been reluctant to approach her. He's decided today is the day:

John: "Hi, there. I've seen you studying here before. Looks like you have a lot of reading to do for psychology."

Emily: "Yeah, I have a presentation tomorrow."

John: "I'd be happy to be your test audience if you need to practice."

Emily: "I'm OK, but thanks anyway."

John: "Well, I'm John; it's nice to meet you.

Emily: "I'm Emily, and that's very nice of you, but I prefer studying alone. See you around!"

John: "All right, Emily. Maybe another time you'll let me suffer through psychology homework with you."

John approached Emily confidently and made observant comments that indicated his interest. While he didn't get an invitation to join her, he broke the ice and will feel more comfortable around Emily the next time he sees her. In the next chapter you'll see how John could have kept the conversation going even longer.

Just to recap: In this chapter we learned that the keys to getting started are appearing confident (even if you have to fake this at first), knowing how to initiate a conversation and introducing or re-introducing yourself. Now you're ready to have a conversation!

POKE → Grab your chisel and start breaking the ice; your insecurities will start to melt away.

CHAPTER 4

SURFING FOR MORE:
Simple ways to keep the conversation going

Now that you know how to approach someone, you need to be able to keep the conversation going and make it interesting. Think of a time when you've arrived early to class and struck up a conversation with another student. What happens when you struggle through the small talk, only to realize that class still hasn't begun and you're out of sparkling conversation? Or imagine sitting at Thanksgiving dinner next to Uncle Jerry, who's only giving one-word answers to your questions. In this chapter you'll find some keys to unlocking the secret of how to keep the conversation in play!

The best way to move a conversation forward after you break the ice is to "**TALK**": **Try** a compliment, **Ask** questions, **Listen** well, and **Keep** your surroundings in mind.

To start "**TALK**"ing:

TRY offering a compliment. Genuine praise and favorable remarks always put people at ease. Once someone feels good, it is easier for that person to open up and stay involved in a conversation.

For example, if you are visiting someone's home for the first time you might say: "Your room looks great! Where did you get the idea to paint your walls like that?"

Or if you want to start a dialogue with your new history teacher you could try: "I really like when you encourage class discussions. It gives me a chance to speak my mind and hear other people's thoughts on the subject."

ASK questions. If you hit a quiet spot in the conversation, follow up with questions. This is a great way to show your interest and keep the dialogue going.

For example: If you're talking to another student during study group and a lull occurs in the conversation you could ask: "How did you come up with that idea (for the year-end English paper)?" or "What do you think we should've done differently (on the group project that received a low grade)?"

If you're having dinner at a relative's house and chitchat has come to an awkward pause try a question like: "Is anyone going on any trips this summer? Anything special you're looking forward to?" or "How did you communicate with friends when you were my age? Strictly by phone or did you just hang out?"

While chatting with someone you know is on the wrestling team, you might revive a dying conversation with a question about something you know they'll talk about, like: "What do you do during wrestling practice?"

LISTEN. There's a reason we have two ears and only one mouth—spending more time listening than talking is one of the secrets to successful conversation! When you're actually listening to someone speak instead of worrying about what you might say next, you'll hear things mentioned that you can use in follow-up statements or questions.

Show you're listening to someone by prompting them with responses and follow-up questions to things they've said, such as: "Wow, it sounds like you had such a good time! What was your favorite part of the trip?" or "What happened next?"

Avoid using generic affirmations that might make you seem uninterested such as "oh, yeah?" and "uh-huh," unless you're showing sincerity in other ways, such as with nonverbal cues. Samples of body language you can use to indicate that you're interested and listening include nodding, smiling and looking the other person in the eye (more on nonverbal communication later).

KEEP the occasion and the surroundings in mind. Take the time to notice what's going on around you so you can use this information during your conversation.

For example, if the conversation lags while you and a date are waiting for a movie you could say, "Have you seen this actor in anything before?"

At a job interview, take notice of the surroundings. During a pause in conversation, you might say: "Tell me about the trophy on your desk—I bet there's a good story behind it!"

If you're running out of things to say to someone at a party, you can point out something interesting about the room: "Did you notice the dog bed? There must be a dog to match it somewhere around here. Do you like animals?"

Let's take a look at the TALK approach in action:

My friend Kristy has a teenage daughter, Kendra. Kendra has an interest in culinary arts and wants to get a summer job at a little neighborhood restaurant near her home. She always walks by it and notices the appealing food but is reluctant to apply for a job. However, recently she went into the restaurant and began a conversation with the manager, Trisha. Here was their dialogue:

Trisha: "Hi. Can I help you?"

Kendra: "Yes, hi, my name is Kendra. I live around the corner and was wondering if you're hiring for the summer? I love this restaurant, especially the weekly specials. They always have such creative ingredients!"

Trisha: "It's nice to meet you, Kendra, I'm Trisha the manager. We will probably be hiring some extra help for the summer."

Kendra: "Would you mind telling me what kind of employee you're looking for?"

Trisha: "Someone with a flexible schedule who's open to doing all types of tasks in both the back and front of the house. We need someone who can seat people, bus tables, and run food all in the same shift."

Kendra: "It would be great to learn it all! And a position like that would teach me so much about the restaurant business."

Trisha: "Can I see your résumé?"

Kendra: "Absolutely, here it is."

Trisha: "Oh, you go to Wayne Prep High School? I went there, too! Well, it's been a few years. Are Mrs. Collins and Mr. Thomas still there? They were my favorites!"

Kendra: "They're both still there. I have Mr. Thomas for statistics right now. Did you like Wayne Prep? Were you ever in Cooking Club?"

Trisha: "I really liked high school, but cooking was not on my mind back then."

Kendra: "I love going to school there, but I can't wait to graduate and go to college."

Trisha: "Where are you looking to go?"

Kendra: "I only really want to go to one school—the Art Institute of California in San Diego to study cooking."

Trisha: "That's where I went! They have a fantastic culinary program."

Kendra: "Oh, wow, that's so cool. I really want to focus on Italian cuisine. What was your specialty?"

Trisha: "Italian— and I'm learning even more by working as the manager here."

Kendra: "That's great! Oh, wow (pointing to a photo on the wall), is that the chef?"

Trisha: "Yes, that's Chef Lorenzo with his signature pasta Carbonara."

Kendra: "That's my favorite dish here. He knows how to mix the flavors just perfectly."

Trisha: "He's one of the best chefs I know."

Kendra: "Well, I'd love to experience working in a great restaurant like this. I'd like to learn as much as I can before I head off to college. Thank you so much for taking a few moments to speak with me."

Trisha: "No problem. Thanks for dropping off your résumé! I will be in touch next week once we figure out our staffing needs for the summer."

As you can see, Kendra's use of TALK helped her carry on a conversation with Trisha. She was also able to make meaningful connections that they can use in the future, such as the fact that Trisha attended the same high school, had some of the same teachers, and that Kendra is interested in going to the same college Trisha attended. Because Kendra asked questions about Trisha, listened to her answers, noticed her surroundings and seemed genuinely interested, the conversation was able to unfold naturally. Kendra ended up getting the job and was able to make a friend.

Now, remember John and Emily from the last chapter? John did a good job of approaching Emily and breaking the ice, but he let the conversation die too soon. Here is how he could have kept the conversation moving forward by listening, asking questions and making observations.

John: "Hi, there. I've seen you studying here before. Looks like you have a lot of reading to do for psychology."

Emily: "Yeah, I have a presentation tomorrow."

John: "I'd be happy to be your test audience if you need to practice."

Emily: "I'm OK, but thanks anyway."

John: "Well, I'm John, and it would just make my week if you'd let me help you practice."

Emily: "I'm Emily, and that's very nice of you, but I prefer studying alone. See you around!"

John: "All right, Emily. Maybe another time you'll let me suffer through psychology homework with you. Hey, I really like your Antlers T-shirt."

Emily: "Thanks, I see them in concert every time they come through."
John: "Me, too! Are you going to the show next month?"
Emily: "Of course. Are you?"
John: "I wouldn't miss it. Maybe we can go together?"
Emily: "Well, I'm going with some friends already. But maybe we can meet up at the show."
John: "That sounds good. I'm actually going to see this local band tomorrow night at a small venue downtown. They have a similar sound to The Antlers. Would you be interested in coming with me?"
Emily: "That sounds fun. Thanks!"

It may be a huge coincidence that John and Emily share a similar passion for a band. So let's think about how John could have handled this scenario if Emily weren't wearing an Antlers T-shirt.

John: "Hi there. I've seen you studying here before. Looks like you have a lot of reading to do for psychology."
Emily: "Yeah, I have a presentation tomorrow."
John: "I'd be happy to be your test audience if you need to practice."
Emily: "I'm OK, but thanks anyway."
John: "Well, I'm John, and it would just make my week if you'd let me help you practice."
Emily: "I'm Emily, and that's very nice of you, but I prefer studying alone. See you around!"
John: "All right, Emily. I make a really good audience, but I understand. So, will you be studying here tomorrow? Maybe I can convince you to take a break and buy you a cup of coffee?"
Emily: "I'm not really sure. It depends on my schedule. But that sounds like fun."

John: "Can I give you my email address? You could let me know what time would work for you, and we could go from there."
Emily: "Sounds good."
John: "Great! Good luck with your presentation."
Emily: "Thanks!"

John was persistent and confident, which ultimately won him a potential date with Emily. Equally important, he was prepared to keep the conversation going and be a great listener.

Now consider a group of teen girls who are part of a volunteer club outside of school. Chelsea is the only one from her school. She is friendly with the girls but doesn't speak to them much because they're all in established cliques from their designated schools. Every week the volunteer program takes on a new project for a few hours. This week participants are planting trees at the local park. Chelsea has decided to attempt to get to know a group of three girls from a neighboring school using her "TALK" skills.

Chelsea: "Hi there. I'm Chelsea from Ponderosa High.
Madison: "Hi. I'm Madison, and this is Samira and Nina. We go to Washington High."
Chelsea: "Cool. You guys have a good baseball team."
Nina: "Yeah, they're pretty good."
Chelsea: "I love your nails. Hope you don't mess them up too bad while planting."
Samira: "Thanks. The color is Lip Smack. We all painted our nails together last weekend. Don't you love working in the park?"

Chelsea: "Yeah. I'm so glad to be outside. What else are you guys involved in at school?"

Madison: "I'm in the band, and Samira and Nina are in French Club."

Chelsea: "That's great. I'm taking my third year of French. I can't wait to go to France to practice. Have either of you been there?"

Nina: "I went last summer. It's wonderful. You'll be practically fluent by the time you leave."

Chelsea: "Great! Maybe you can help me practice?"

Samira: "OK. We're always trying to speak it as much as possible. Oui? (Yes?)"

Chelsea: "Moi aussi! (Me, too!)"

Chelsea did a great job of introducing herself and giving her target conversation partners a compliment upfront. This automatically made the group of girls more at ease and allowed them to see that Chelsea was non-threatening and genuine. From there, Chelsea capitalized on a common interest and was able to listen and ask follow-up questions. She also left the door open for further interaction in the near future.

By utilizing these techniques, you'll be a pro at talking to people of all ages and with different interests. Treat each interaction like a long-distance race during which you have to pace yourself and stay focused—rather than a sprint—and you'll be a communication winner every time.

POKE → If ever in doubt about keeping a conversation going, remember, all you have to do is "**TALK**": Try a compliment, Ask questions, Listen well, and Keep your surroundings in mind.

CHAPTER 5

DIGGING DEEPER:
*Using open-ended questions to improve the
quality of the conversation*

Let's talk just a little bit more about questions. It's important to understand that all questions aren't created equal. Some will help you further the conversation, while others will quickly bring it to a close. In order to keep things rolling, build rapport and connect with people, you'll want to use open-ended questions instead of closed-ended questions.

An open-ended question is the sort of query that requires more than a one-word response. It prompts your conversation partner to elaborate on his or her thoughts. For instance, if you ask: "How was the game?" it's likely you'll hear an answer such as "Great" or "OK" in response. Similarly, if you ask: "What's up?" you're certain to get a common answer such as "Nothing" or "Not much." However, if you ask, "What did you like about the game today?" or "What was on the biology test today?" you'll more likely get a longer answer.

While the first questions in the above paragraph were closed-ended questions, the second were open-ended. Examples of open-ended questions that work (almost every time!) include:

- "Tell me about (your summer, the tournament, your date, your vacation)."
- "What should I do to get ready for (the test, camping trip, audition, try-outs)?"
- "What was (that trip abroad, that concert, growing up here, working there) like for you?"
- "How did you come up with that (essay, outfit, dance routine, blog post)?"
- "What has been going on with your (job, family, studies)?"
- "Bring me up to date on your (college applications, girlfriend, music library, job hunt)."
- "What do you think about (the current event, the political candidate, the news article, that new invention)?"
- "Why do you think (the *American Idol* contestant was eliminated, William Faulkner wrote like that, the teacher was so late, Sarah broke up with David, the school is imposing a new rule)?"

All of the above open-ended questions inspire responses that will help you continue a conversation. Once you get the initial information, you can dig even deeper.

If you stumble into a conversation by accidentally using a closed-ended question, you can easily salvage the situation by offering follow-up questions. For example, falling into a lazy pattern, I asked my friend Joni, "How was your day?" She replied, "Great," then the conversation evaporated. I had begun with a closed-ended question, and Joni didn't think I really cared about her day. By digging deeper, however, I could still show I was interested and invite more meaningful conversation. I could say, for example, "What made it great?" or "What did you have going on today?"

Whenever you begin a dialogue with a closed-ended question, be ready to dig deeper so the other person knows you're interested in hearing more. Here are some examples of how to do this:

Mary: "How was your final?"
Darius: "Tough."
Mary: "What was hard about it?"

Mary: "How were your holidays?"
Darius: "Pretty good."
Mary: "What kinds of things did you do?"

The following dialogues show an extension of the same idea:

Kenny: "How was your weekend?"
Amir: "Good."
Kenny: "What did you do?"
Amir: "My brother visited from college."
Kenny: "Where does he go to college? Does he like it there?"

Teisha: "What's up?"
Sam: "Nothing."
Teisha: "What are you doing today?"
Sam: "Going home, doing some homework. Might go out later."
Teisha: "Where do you like to go out? What do you like to do?"

How many times has your mom or dad asked you after school: "How was your day?" I bet it didn't take long before that question meant "Hello" and nothing more. It's not that your parents don't care about your day, it's that the question can become so automatic that it morphs into more of a greeting than a true query. Without a follow-up question, the conversation is likely to end, and your parents won't learn much about your day. Follow-up (and more profound) questions keep the conversation going and show a genuine interest.

Don't forget that this is a two-way street. If someone asks you a question and is obviously interested in your response, it's polite to answer in a way the keeps the conversation flowing. To do this, avoid being a poor sport and be willing to disclose information about yourself.

The poor sport is someone who's not interested in keeping the conversation ball in play. He always finds a way to reduce a beautiful question into a simple one-word answer. When asked, *"What did you do this weekend?"* the poor sport will reply with, *"Nothing."* When prompted, *"How was your train trip across Europe?"* he or she will answer, *"Good."* Both questions leave plenty of room for the poor sport to select some aspect of the weekend or train trip to mention for the sake of the conversation. Instead, he opts to end the conversation by holding the ball instead of passing it back. The poor sport just doesn't play well with others. *"How are you?"* someone might ask. The poor sport responds: *"Fine."* Which often really means:

F: Frustrated

I: Irritated

N: Not interested in talking

E: Exhausted

Instead of taking this approach, be a good sport and respond with even a small disclosure that can keep the conversation alive. For example:

"How are you?"

"Thanks for asking, I'm really enjoying the book we're reading for American Lit."

"How was your train trip across Europe?"

"It was amazing—I must have taken thousands of pictures."

"What did you do this weekend?"

"I mostly just hung out and played video games, but I did go out to lunch with Brandon."

"I played disc golf."

"My dad and I worked on his 1967 Mustang."

Here are two other examples:

Say you're working a shift behind the counter at the bakery. Instead of taking this approach....

Customer: "How's your shift going?"
You: "OK."

(This conversation is dead. You have just killed it.)

...Try this:

Customer: "How is work going?"
You: "Not bad. I just rang up one of those cakes with a photo printed in the icing; those are so cool! And I should get out just in time to catch a movie with some friends."

Or perhaps the coach approaches you. Instead of taking this approach...

Coach: "How's your summer been?"
You: "OK."
...Try this:
Coach: "How's your summer been?"
You: "My summer's been good. I went to a science camp for a week."
Or: *"It was OK. I got a new bike I'm pretty excited about."*

Now you've given insight into your life so the coach can get to know you better and can follow up with questions about science camp or where you like to ride your bike.

POKE → Pose open-ended questions and answer by disclosing information about yourself to keep dialogue wide open.

CHAPTER 6

CRASHING:

Eight ways to kill a conversation

Once you've got a conversation rolling, you might think you're in for easy sailing and the conversation will continue to flow. But a conversation can be like a moving train, and you must always be on the alert not to say something that will stop it in its tracks.

You've probably been in a situation in which a conversation has been moving along but suddenly begins to feel like a power struggle over who can talk the most or tell the longest stories. Or maybe you've been nervous and trying to think of things to say and inadvertently said something embarrassing. Such missteps are understandable and often go unnoticed by others, but there are things you can do to avoid such awkward moments. If you want to be a smooth conversationalist, here are some things to avoid:

1) Interrogating your conversational partner.

Maybe you saw the episode of the TV show The Big Bang Theory in which Sheldon came up with a 211-question survey to screen candidates for the position of his new friend. While questions are a great way to get to know new people, don't get carried away. You're not conducting an FBI interrogation, you're trying to encourage a free-flowing exchange of thoughts and ideas. An interrogation might go something like this:

> Mateo: "How was that concert last night?"
> Joel: "Pretty good."
> Mateo: "What did you like about it?"
> Joel: "The band. They had some good songs."
> Mateo: "Which songs did you like best?"
> Joel: "I don't know. There was one about California that was pretty cool."
> Mateo: "Can you remember the name of it?"
> Joel: "No. . . ."

And so on. Mateo could have taken a better approach by offering some information of his own when he realized Joel wasn't going to be forthcoming with stories about the concert. The conversation might have gone more like this:

> Mateo: "How was that concert last night?"

Joel: "Pretty good."

Mateo: "What did you like about it?"

Joel: "The band. They had some pretty good songs."

Mateo: "I hear them on the radio a lot lately. They seem to be getting big. I think I'll start with their first album and see if I like it."

Joel: "No way—start with their newest. It took them a few years to hit their stride, but now they're putting out some real quality stuff. They remind me a lot of The Black Keys."

Mateo: "I love The Black Keys...."

Now Mateo and Joel have more to talk about. They've broadened the conversation beyond the concert and opened it up to talking about other bands they like. When your questions keep receiving short answers, it's a good idea to switch gears from interrogation to sharing information.

2) Getting too personal too fast.

Avoid asking questions that hit on delicate topics, such as: "How much money do you make at that job?" or "Why do your parents look so different from you?" The same goes for sharing sensitive information with someone you just met: "Hi. I'm Henry. We put our pet ferret to sleep yesterday."

Sometimes you may want to know something personal and feel like it's an appropriate question to ask in the situation. For instance, if you're talking to someone who works at the place where you're applying for a job, you may really want to know how much he gets paid. Or maybe you're trying to deepen a friendship with someone and feel like it might be appropriate to tell that person something personal about yourself. In this case, don't start the conversation with the personal information and do give the person notice that you're going to cross the line from casual to serious. Also, give them the option not to answer a personal question—if they're uncomfortable, they'll be grateful you gave them the "out." In the following example, Amber wants to know how much she stands to make at a bookstore she wants to work at.

Amber: *"Thanks for talking to me about your work. I think I'd really like it there."*

Tia: *"It's awesome. It's usually pretty slow, but the manager doesn't mind if you do your homework when there aren't any customers around. I hope you apply."*

Amber: *"Do you mind if I ask a personal question? You don't have to answer if you don't want to."*

Tia: *"That's OK—what do you want to ask?"*

Amber: *"I'm wondering how much you make working there?"*

Notice how Amber gave Tia the option not to answer and prepared Tia for a serious question. In the next example, Sara wants to share her struggles with dyslexia with her friendLucas.

Lucas: *"How are you doing in English? I love that class."*

Sara: *"I've always kind of struggled with it. Can I share something with you that's kind of personal, and trust you not to tell others about it? If you don't feel comfortable hearing about it, then that's fine. I won't take it personally."*

Lucas: *"I can keep it to myself—what did you want to tell me?"*

Sara gave Lucas a heads-up and laid out her condition for sharing the information—he couldn't talk about it to others. This way, Lucas understood that what was coming was both personal and private, and was given the option to not hear it.

3) Turning conversation into a competitive sport.

Don't try to top the other person's story. When your new lab partner tells you how he broke his leg, for example, resist the urge to detail the snowboarding accident that left you in a body cast. And don't fall prey to the match game: you know, your friend tells you about the fun vacation her family took to Disneyland and you interrupt to let her know you've already visited there and enjoyed Disneyland as well. You might as well simply cut her off with: "Been there, done that."

Sometimes it's good to establish shared interests and experiences, but give the other person a chance to tell their story before jumping in with yours. And watch out for matching every one of their stories with one of your own, or you'll start to sound like an endlessly echoing "Me too, me too."

4) Interrupting.

Let the other person finish his or her thought. It shows that you are listening and considering that person's ideas, rather than simply planning what you will say next. If you ever do get caught up in your own thoughts and stop listening, it's usually not rude to ask the other person to repeat or clarify what they said. More often than not, they'll be happy that you're making an effort to really listen and understand.

5) Hogging the spotlight.

Remember to pass the conversation ball, rather than talking for a prolonged period of time without a break. The frame-by-frame account of the video you downloaded with the in-line skaters doing crazy tricks on the rooftop of a building should wait until you are better acquainted with your conversation partner, or until you're certain he or she will not be put to sleep by such a vivid and detailed account.

6) Giving advice without being asked.

Leave that to your parents. No one wants to hear your advice on swinging a golf club, keeping up with fashion or what sorority is the best unless that advice has been solicited. If you feel like someone might benefit from your knowledge or suggestions, ask them first if they want to hear it and make sure they know they have the option to say "no."

7) Gossiping.

This is not cool. You can find topics of conversation that don't involve speaking badly about others. Most gossip starts out with "Did you hear about Jodi?" or "Do you know where Steven has been or who he's been with?"

It is far too easy to fall into the trap of talking badly about others, especially in school or work situations where everyone has something to say about other people. Starting conversations with things like, *"Danny always wears the worst clothes," "I can't stand the way Michelle eats," or "Did you hear about Ms. Hanson's new boyfriend?"* just makes you look shallow, and even mean. If you find yourself in a conversation in which people are bad-mouthing others, show your distaste by walking away or finding something nice to say. Other people might even take your cue and switch to more positive conversation topics.

8) Suffering from foot-in-mouth disease.

Uncle Stu asks Ali if he got into the University of Indiana and, in front of the entire holiday dinner table, Ali is faced with divulging that he, in fact, did not gain acceptance to that fine institution. Or someone asks if Lizzy changed her hair color for a particular reason, or why Stan's dad is home all day. All of these present potentially awkward and uncomfortable moments. Although we cannot control others, it is up to us to learn from the above examples and not ask personal questions to which we don't already know the answers. It's best to zip lips before landing a foot squarely inside one's mouth.

POKE → Don't go down a conversation path you think could lead to any type of harm.

CHAPTER 7

LOGGING OFF:
Tactful ways to end a conversation

Ending a conversation can be awfully awkward. It's tempting sometimes to keep a conversation going by forcing questions and rambling on and on, but you can usually sense when a conversation has run its course and it's time to bid farewell. There will be more pauses, some roaming gazes and perhaps a few "so's" or "umms". The idea is to get out before anyone begins to feel uncomfortable in a conversation.

The most effective way to conclude a chat is to bring it full circle. Recall why you started talking with this individual and close with a direct statement, for example: "I'm glad we got to walk through our class presentation" or, "Thanks for talking to me about the sorority's charity efforts." By making a meaningful summation, you remind that person about why you were conversing in the first place.

When doing this, it's always a good idea to show appreciation for their input. You might try:

"Great to see you and hear about your college visits."

"It's been interesting talking with you about politics."

"Thanks for your advice about college applications—I'll definitely use it!"

"It's great talking with someone who knows so much about open-source software."

"Thanks for telling me about that author. I love a good recommendation!"

"It's really interesting to hear more about your family."

"I'm so glad you introduced me to Jason. I'm finally getting around to meeting some new people."

"It's great to talk with someone else who watches <u>South Park</u>."

Another way to exit the conversation is to be prepared with some closing statements. The following useful exit lines allow you to excuse yourself gracefully and politely. They won't offend or make your conversation partner feel uncomfortable.

- *"I need to catch someone over there before they leave, but thanks for chatting with me."*
- *"I'm going to grab a bite to eat. It was nice talking to you!"*
- *"I hope you'll excuse me; I want to talk to my math teacher about our assignment."*
- *"I guess I should circulate and meet some of the new members of the chapter."*
- *"I want to see if there are any other people from my major here today."*
- *"I want to meet some of my other friends' parents while they're still around."*

- *"I don't want to be late for class, but I'll see you after school."*
- *"I promised myself I'd meet at least three new people before I leave."*
- *"I want to make my way around and say hello to everyone."*
- *"I've been dying to meet that person, so I'm going to go introduce myself."*
- *"I'm going to join some of my friends in the courtyard for lunch. You're welcome to join us if you want."*
- *"My ride is waiting to pick me up, but I'll see you in class tomorrow."*
- *"I need some more punch. Do you want anything to drink?"*

None of these excuses offers up an artificial reason that could be interpreted as insulting. By placing the emphasis on you—by using words such as "I need" or "I want"—you will avoid offending your conversation counterpart. For instance, you wouldn't want to say to someone, "You don't seem to have much more to say about it. It was nice to chat!" or "You're really interesting, gotta go" or "Weren't you on your way to class?" or "Well, you have to go to that movie, sooo. . . ."

One warning: now that you've told this individual what you need, want or are going to do, you must follow through. If you said you were going to leave the baseball game, for example, don't get caught chatting and laughing with a group of people on the bleachers nearby. If your previous conversation partner sees you aren't really leaving, he'll be offended and you could strain a relationship that you've worked hard to develop. Lots of times we really do want to "go grab a drink," but on the way there, we run into another friend. If this happens, say hello to your friend and let that person know you will be right back once you grab that drink you intended to retrieve. Always honor the exit line you used to ensure that no feelings are hurt.

Another strategy for leaving a conversation is to ask for help or direction. If you're at a gathering and are having a conversation you wish to end, you might ask: "Do you know anyone else here majoring in criminal justice? I would like to get some tips." If your conversation partner supplies guidance, such as: "You should talk to Alessandra; she started the program last year," you can then tell her that you're headed over to Alessandra. If the response is "no," you can explain that you're off to find someone who might be able to help you.

Other examples of asking for help include:

"Is there anybody that you know here who participates in Amnesty International? I would like to learn more about it."

"Who else has had the same experience with this coach?"

"Do you know someone who pledged a sorority last year? I need some pointers."

"Do you know anyone who can give me advice about the SATs?"

"I had hoped to find someone who (is a college recruiter, has ties to the fraternity, is on the host committee, entered the contest, is a year ahead of me in class) this evening. Do you know anyone like that?"

"Where should I go to find about more about (insert topic)?"

"Could you point me towards the snack table?"

"Is there anyone else here that I could speak to about joining the Interact Club?"

If you're still stymied about ending a conversation and sense that your conversation partner will feel abandoned by your exit, ask him or her to join you. You might say:

"Would you like to go to the buffet and grab some food?"

"I need to talk to a teammate. You're welcome to come along."

"I see someone from my high school that I want to say 'Hi' to. Would you care to join me?"

"I was thinking about seeing what that group is talking about. Want to come along?"

Your conversation partner now has a choice: she or he can join you or stay. Either way, you're once again able to move around the room.

Remember, you can harm a relationship if you say the wrong thing or leave a conversation at an inappropriate time. You don't want to be rude, and you don't want to create an uncomfortable situation, because you never know when you might see a person again.

Here are some examples of what NOT to say:

"I see my friends in the corner; I'm going to talk to them."

"I have to take this call." (Unless you really do have to. Even then, your conversation partner may automatically assume you're lying, so take a second to explain why the call is important.)

"Did you see where that gorgeous girl went?"

"I think fraternities are a waste of time, so I'm going to excuse myself."

"I have to check my Facebook."

"Gotta go...."

"It's time for my next tweet. See you later."

As for being on the receiving end of someone else's abrupt or lame attempt to wind down a conversation, keep in mind that while you may have the graciousness to plan your courteous exits, others might not be so kind. Don't take it personally if they say something that seems rude or sudden. Keep your reaction positive.

Let's say, for instance, that you're talking to Lucas about a school project and working out the logistics of a time you'll be able to work on it when he says, "Oh, I have some buddies over at the other lunch table. See you later." He didn't give you the information you needed about the project before starting to walk away, so it's up to you to make a quick close to the conversation. Say, "Sounds good. I'll call you tonight about who will take what parts of the project."

An exit to a conversation is as meaningful as a first impression. You always want to leave on a high note so the next time you interact with that individual it's smooth, comfortable and the groundwork for building on the relationship has already been laid.

POKE → When leaving a conversation, always have an exit strategy, don't forget to express appreciation for what you have learned or heard and keep it classy.

CHAPTER 8

SENDING INSTANT MESSAGES:
How your body language silently communicates with others

OK, multiple-choice test: What is nonverbal communication?

A) A Britney Spears song?

B) An ancient way cavemen spoke to each other?

C) A secret branch of the CIA?

D) The gestures, postures and facial expressions by which a person communicates with others?

If you chose D, you are correct!

Possessing strong nonverbal communication skills is just as important as having verbal aptitude. A dialogue is more than words being thrown back and forth; it also includes physical movements that enhance the conversation. Would you play baseball without a bat? Let's hope not. Just as the bat is essential to playing a baseball game, body language is crucial to a successful interaction.

Gestures, postures and facial expressions are key to any in-person exchange. Those who look alert, relaxed and eager appear open to communication. A nonchalant, unresponsive person often seems aloof and unfriendly. Someone nervously fidgeting or with slumped shoulders looks uninviting. Smiling and making eye contact across the lunch table is a good way to indicate you want to engage with your peers. The same goes for when you're talking to someone, whether it's a teacher, love interest or group partner. It's far better to nod, smile and make eye contact than to appear uninterested. Such simple gestures can make you incredibly likeable and take you from invisible to invincible.

Let's look at a situation with Tyler. Tyler is a sophomore who plays on the junior varsity basketball team at school. He's typically pretty passive. He often sits on the bench and looks down. He never talks to his coach. Tyler is a talented player but because of his reserved nature, he doesn't get as much playing time as others. A shift in his physical behavior—cheering, smiling, high-fiving and using eye contact with his teammates and coach—would better demonstrate to all that he's connected and enjoying being on the team.

Here's how Tyler might raise his profile with the coach and improve his playing time on the team:

Tyler (with his head high and eyes on the coach's eyes): "Coach, I'd really like some more playing time. I've been working really hard in practice. I know some of the guys on the team are older, but I think I deserve a chance to show you what I'm capable of."

Coach: "You show a lot of potential, but I'm not sure you're ready to play at this level yet."

Tyler (with a smile and look of sincerity): "I'm ready, Coach. Just give me a chance."

Coach: "OK, we'll see what you've got next game."

Tyler: Thanks, Coach *(he reaches out and shakes the coach's hand).*

In that scenario, Tyler did not remain invisible and quietly hope the coach would notice him. Instead, he approached his coach confidently. It wasn't necessarily his words that made him stand out but his body language: standing with his shoulders back, making direct eye contact, smiling. It signaled that he is intense, passionate and eager to play. Displaying confidence requires being visible.

Your nonverbal communication cues can make you seem more friendly and approachable. Imagine you're at a busy coffee shop and you realize there aren't any open tables, so you'll have to ask someone to share theirs. You notice a man on his laptop, hunched over and frowning. You see a woman poring over a pile of textbooks, a look of frustration on her face. Then you spot another woman, and she is smiling a little to herself and sitting up straight as she glances around the coffee shop. Who are you going to ask?

Consider another situation: Kristen is very shy and avoids classroom presentations whenever possible. When the teacher poses a question to the class, Kristen always looks away. She's not an active participant in her class. As a result, she comes across as disengaged and is not fully reaching her communication potential. She's letting her fear get in the way of her success as a student.

In order to harness her nonverbal communication skills and engage with people, Kristen needs to look her teacher in the eye and display facial expressions that show she's aware of what's going on in the class. By nodding along as a teacher explains a process, Kristen will signify that she's interested in the teacher's lessons. A soft smile shows the teacher that Kristen heard something that was interesting or amusing to her, and is a welcome sight for any teacher. By contrast, even if it's unintended, a passive face—or worse, a frown—will not warrant a positive reaction from an instructor. Kristen needs to practice showing enthusiasm and participating as much as possible. The repetition will help her develop positive habits. The best way to get past her fear of speaking up in class is to start speaking up. Actively practicing nodding, smiling, sitting up straight and raising her hand in class will help her feel comfortable commenting and asking questions, which will in turn ingratiate her with any instructor. There's a natural connection between appearing engaged and actually being engaged, so start practicing!

Here's a grid to better explain how nonverbal cues translate to others:

Nonverbal cues that work in your favor

Eye Contact	Suggests you're interested and connecting with the individual
Smile	Makes you seem genuine, friendly and approachable
Nod/Head Shake	Shows you're actively participating in a dialogue exchange and are listening

Nonverbal cues that work against you

Crossed Arms or Legs	Indicates you're bored and defensive
Engaging in Other Tasks	Implies you're more interested in other tasks than in the person who's talking to you
Fiddling	Demonstrates lack of interest and engagement

View the following diagrams of positive and negative body language and determine which you most often display.

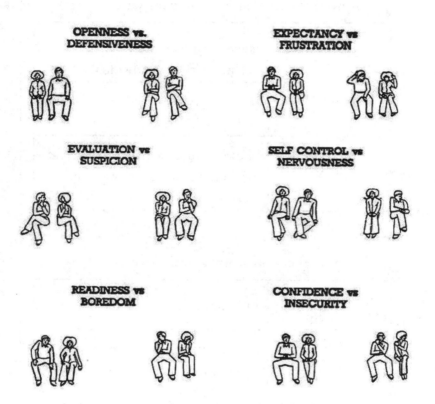

Obviously, those on the right are challenged at executing positive body language, though they may not realize it. Many times, we're unaware of our own body language. Think about it: When you interact with someone who appears ill at ease, eyes darting around the room, shoulders slumped, limp handshake, do you think he or she is doing this on purpose? Suppose you spot a woman across the room whose eyes are focused on the floor and who's wringing her hands continually? Do you think she's aware of her off-putting body language? My guess is that she has no idea. Many of us stand around at meetings and parties with our arms folded across our chests because we find it a comfortable stance. Unfortunately, others often think this posture indicates someone who is a "know-it-all" or arrogant.

Make a conscious effort to work on your body language. With this chapter in mind, consider your habits. Are you aware of your posture, eye contact and what your hands are doing? Make it your mission to focus on your body language in order to see yourself the way the world sees you.

POKE → Don't let your nonverbal communication go out with a whimper—practice projecting confidence and approachability with your gestures, posture and facial expressions. Remember it's not always what you say but the attitude you convey that communicates the loudest.

CHAPTER 9

UPLOADING HONESTY:
*How to impress others and remain true
to yourself*

When did you last change your hair, buy a piece of clothing, try out for a team or join a club because you thought it would be your ticket to acceptance?

I know what it's like to be a teenager; after all, I was one (and I've raised a few, too)! I was shy and lacked confidence. I understand that feeling of wanting to pretend you're someone you're not just to be accepted and recognized by seemingly more self-assured teens. But creating a persona just to fit in won't help you become successful in life. Those who learn to be genuine will have more quality friends, a more positive outlook on life and be more successful in building lasting and meaningful relationships. Developing disingenuous interaction skills during these formative years will only hinder you down the road, when you go on a job interview or a date. If you want to win someone's attention, it's important just to be yourself. Lying, embellishing stories and bragging might get you a temporary buddy, but those tactics won't lead to a long-time, permanent pal. Acting phony might gain you superficial popularity, but it won't yield the kind of satisfying relationships you want. Your teenage years are only a sliver of your existence and by no means define your life. So don't let yourself get sucked into the idea that one misstep will send you off the path of popularity. This is the time to learn how to interact honestly with peers so people learn to trust you are who you say you are and not a phony.

Here are four questions to consider whenever you're initiating any interaction:

1. **Are you worrying about impressing the other person?** If so, consider why this is so important to you. Is it really worth the work to get recognized by this individual?

2. **How will this interaction impact your reputation in the long run?** Be forward-thinking and recognize that some actions you take will follow you.

3. **Are you upholding the integrity of your image while projecting the kind of person you want to be?** Are you being you? It's OK to want to change and adapt, but if this isn't who you are at your core you'll never succeed at leaving the right impression, one that paves the way for an authentic relationship.

4. **Do you need to lie or brag to get attention from this person?** If so, resist at all costs. At best, you'll compromise your personal identity. At worst, you'll get caught and be remembered as the fakest one in school.

Let's look at this issue further by considering ninth-grader Valeria. She does well academically and is in Student Council, but she is quiet and doesn't get a lot of attention. She would like to have more friends. Her classmate, Kara, is a well-known cheerleader and also a Student Council member. Valeria would like to get to know Kara better and spend more time with her social circle. In this first dialogue between them, notice how hard she tries to impress Kara:

Valeria: "Hi Kara! I love your book bag!"
Kara: "Thanks. I got it in New York."
Valeria: "Really? My mom and I are going there this summer. We're staying at a really famous hotel and eating at all these fancy restaurants. I can't wait to go shopping—I hear they have the best stores. When we go on trips we always get treated like celebrities because my mom has lots of connections."
Kara: "Cool. Hope you have a good time."

In that encounter, Valeria completely inflated her comments as she tried to sound more interesting to Kara. Instead of winning Kara over, though, she turned her off and discouraged any further conversation.

Valeria could have said this:
Valeria: "Hi Kara! I love your book bag!"

Kara: "Thanks. I got it in New York."

Valeria: "Really? I'm going to New York this summer with my mom. Could you tell me about your favorite places there?"

Kara: "Oh, I'd love to talk about New York. If you want to get together this weekend, I'll show you my pictures."

This response keeps the conversation going and allows Kara to engage with Valeria. Valeria seems sincere about wanting to know about Kara's experience in New York, which makes her more likable than when she's just boasting about herself to get attention. Valeria has made a favorable impression.

Let's consider another example. Patrick is a tenth-grade basketball player, but he's shy and hasn't made friends with his teammates. He sees an opportunity before practice one day to strike up a conversation with the point guard on his team, Malik. As you read the following conversation, note that Patrick really does enjoy video games but is not very good at skateboarding.

Patrick: "Hi, Malik. Did you do anything fun over the weekend?"

Malik: "I don't know. I went skateboarding."

Patrick: "Oh, man, I love skateboarding. I go all the time on the weekends. Have you played the new skateboarding video game?"

Malik: "Nah, I don't really like video games."

Patrick: "Yeah, me neither."

Malik: "Oh. See you at practice!"

Did you notice how Patrick agreed with everything Malik said, even when it wasn't true? Now, if Malik and Patrick do become friends, Patrick will have to continue lying about his interests or admit that he lied in the first place. They may not become friends at all if Malik noticed that Patrick was being fake.

If Patrick had been honest, the conversation might have gone more like this:

Patrick: "Hi, Malik. Did you do anything fun over the weekend?
Malik: "I don't know. I went skateboarding."
Patrick: "Oh, yeah? I like playing skateboarding video games, but I've never been very good at the real thing. Are you pretty good?"
Malik: "Yeah. I could probably teach you a thing or two, if you wanted to come to the skateboard park with me."

This time, by being honest, Patrick got an offer to hang out with his new friend and a chance to learn something new. He didn't come off as fake, and he will not have to lie about liking video games or being a novice skateboarder.

Remember, friends you gain by being yourself will be better friends than those who only know the phony you.

Your teen years can be some of the most daunting of your life, or not. The choice is yours. Will you be a genuine person with your own unique opinions to share, or will you try to be someone you're not?

POKE → The easiest way to get through tough times and the process of "finding" yourself is to remember that being yourself is more conducive to long-term relationships than trying to impress others by being someone you're not.

CHAPTER 10

Rebooting Your Approach
With Adults:
Interacting with authority figures in ways that earn their respect

As a teen you might find it tricky to interact with authority figures, especially as you begin striving for independence and control over your own situations and problems. You might feel authority figures are picking on you or being unfair. But in most cases they're only looking out for your best interests. Although you may have moments during which you don't agree with your parents or feel like a teacher or coach is treating you unfairly, you can find ways to earn their respect and address them maturely.

The best way to earn an authority figure's respect is to be respectful of them. Of course, this can be difficult when they're telling you that you can't do something or they make you feel insignificant. But once you've established a rapport with them, they will be much less intimidating to approach or to communicate and interact with. Follow these suggestions and you'll be an authority on addressing authority figures:

- **Make eye contact.** By looking authority figures in the eyes, you show that you're not intimidated by them and that you have confidence.
- **Be respectful.** Listen to their reasoning without interrupting. Speak to them in a soft tone. Avoid whining, using slang and giving off an attitude. The more you respect them, the more they'll respect you.
- **Explain yourself and what you're hoping to accomplish.** If you want a different grade on a test, craft a well thought out explanation of why you deserve it. If you want a pay raise at your job, outline what your responsibilities are and what you're willing to do for more money. Invest the time in crafting your argument rather than simply reacting negatively. The better you can articulate your position, the more likely the authority figure is to consider your point of view.
- **Be assertive.** If your teacher wrongfully accuses you of cheating or your boss incorrectly accuses you of stealing, stand up to them in a respectful and genuine manner. Try: "With all due respect, I didn't cheat on the test, and I would never do something like that. I studied really hard, and I'd appreciate you recognizing my hard work."

Exercise:

Draw up a list of the primary authority figures in your life: parents, teachers, employers, coaches and anyone else with whom you may have frequent contact. Then make a note about your relationship with each of them.

For those with whom you don't always see eye to eye:

1. Consider why you perceive a discord in the relationship. Are you afraid of not living up to their expectations? Do you think they don't understand you? Do you think they're negatively judging you?

2. Think about how you may be able to connect with them and get them to understand you and respect you.

3. Recognize that in some limited cases, an adult may not be a person whose respect is worth attaining.

- **Accept blame when appropriate.** If you made a mistake or did something wrong, own up to it. If, for example, you were assigned to clean your frat house kitchen as one of your chores and you ended up hanging at a friend's apartment instead, your fraternity brothers will be much more understanding if you own up to it. Try: "I ended up going to Adam's place to study and didn't take the time to tackle the kitchen. I know I let you down, and will go clean it right now."

- **Never lie.** Lying will only get you into further trouble, so it's best to be up front and honest. If an authority figure catches you in a lie, that person is much more likely to doubt your credibility from that point on. As a result, he or she will be much more difficult to communicate with in the future.

- **Don't reject discipline.** Many teens fear authority figures because they have the power to discipline them; a teacher can put them in detention, a boss can fire them, a parent can ground them. Remember that most authority figures are trying to teach you life lessons and provide you with guidance. If you feel like the time doesn't match the crime, say, "I understand where you're coming from, and I agree there should be a consequence, but this seems a bit extreme and I think a more appropriate outcome would be X."

- **Appeal to their emotions.** All adults were once teens themselves and can identify with certain situations and emotions that teens go through. If, say, you want to get an extension on turning in a paper, try talking to your teacher on a personal level, for example: "Mr. Johnson, I was wondering if you'd consider giving me a week's extension on this term paper. I worked hard this week to prepare for the concert performance and didn't have enough time to give this paper all the attention it deserves. This was a really important concert for me, but now it's over and I'd really appreciate your understanding."

- **Have a "practice" conversation.** Prior to having an important or potentially intimidating talk with an authority figure, have a "practice" conversation. Write out some bullet points and read them out loud in the mirror or rehearse with a friend. Think about what might could happen in the conversation and even afterwards. This way, you'll be prepared for different scenarios.

Imagine, for instance, having to tell your soccer coach that you want more playing time. His response could be a variety of things, such as: "You're not ready." Or: "If you practice an extra hour a week, you might be ready." Or: "Maybe we'll try it in this weekend's game and see how it goes." It would be to your advantage to have a response prepared for any of these situations so you can achieve your goal. The more you've rehearsed what you want to say in your head, the more confident you'll be saying it out loud. You'll then be prepared to offer a response, such as: "What will it take to prove to you that I'm ready?" Or: "Is it all right with you if I touch base on this before the game on Saturday?"

In the following example, Shannon puts many of these tips to work as she approaches her boss, Destiny, at the local ice cream shop about getting more hours. Shannon knows that Destiny will be resistant to the idea because of a recent conflict Shannon had with a coworker, but because another employee recently left for college, she knows this is the best time to ask for extra shifts.

Shannon: "Hi, Destiny. Do you have a minute to talk to me about my schedule?"

Destiny: "Sure, I have a few minutes."

Shannon: "Well, I'm trying to save up for my school trip to Costa Rica, and it would really help me out if I could get an extra two shifts each week. Now that Stacey has left, could you give me some of her shifts?"

Destiny: "Shannon, I understand why you need the extra hours, but I'm concerned about your communication with coworkers—it isn't always as productive as I'd like. I was thinking about giving the shifts to someone who gets along better with everyone."

Shannon: "I understand, but ever since I had that argument with Paul I've gone out of my way to be respectful towards everyone here. I'm even reading a book about face-to-face communication. If I'm able to prove to you during work this week that I can get along with everyone, will you consider giving me the shifts?"

Destiny: "That sounds reasonable. I do need coverage for Stacey's shifts by next week."

Shannon: "Then can I talk to you about this again on Saturday, before you do the schedule?"

Destiny: "Yes, absolutely. We'll talk more then."

Shannon was both respectful and assertive in this situation, and she took the blame and made an emotional appeal along with laying out a plan for action. Because of her reasoned, mature approach Destiny heard her out and will give her a chance despite initial objections.

Let's look at another situation. Eleventh-grader Daniel feels his teacher has graded him unfairly on a recent presentation because his presentation partner was sick and unable to provide much help. He wants to see if he can get a better grade, so he has practiced going over what he will say to Ms. Chaffin, and now feels ready. He approaches his teacher in this way:

Daniel: "Hi, Ms. Chaffin. I'd like to talk to you about my grade on the PowerPoint presentation."

Ms. Chaffin: "Hello, Daniel. I made it clear when I handed out the assignment that I would grade presentations using the rubric. According to that, you received a B, which is not a bad grade."

Daniel: "I hear you. However, the others worked in pairs and had a better shot at meeting all of the rubric's requirements. I didn't have much help from my partner because he was out sick all week. I created the entire PowerPoint myself and delivered the presentation alone. I don't want my partner to be punished, but couldn't I get extra points for the extra effort I put in?"

Ms. Chaffin: "I can't just go doling out extra points every time a student goes above and beyond. I'm glad you put in the effort in a difficult situation, but unless you can find something in the rubric that would allow you extra points, then you're stuck with the B."

Daniel: "I did look through the rubric and noted the part about 'being prepared and practiced before the presentation.' I got all but two of those points. Could I have those two points?"

Ms. Chaffin: "I suppose you were prepared and practiced, especially considering you had to do it yourself. Yes, Daniel, I'll give you those two points. That would bring you to a B+."

Daniel: "Thank you, Ms. Chaffin. I appreciate you working with me on this."

Daniel persisted in his argument and, because he had practiced beforehand, he was prepared to defend himself with the grading rubric. He was polite, assertive and patient with his reasoning. Though such conversations might not always turn out the way you plan, you'll never know unless you try.

While interacting with authority figures and superiors can be uncomfortable, following these tips will increase your chances for successful encounters—and you may even learn valuable lessons from the adults you would have alienated, lessons you can apply throughout your life.

Have Patience with the Parentals *"You just don't understand!"* *"You're being unreasonable!" "You're ruining my life!"*

Ah, famous phrases said by most teens to their parents at one time or another. At some point such adolescent angst has consumed pretty much anyone who has ever been sixteen. Technology might have dramatically changed, but the fundamentals of parent-adolescent relationships remain the same as they were twenty, thirty, forty years ago. When you're the sixteen-year-old, it feels like no one can relate to your troubles. In reality, though, most parents sympathize with young adults who want freedom and privileges.

Differences are going to arise. But there are a few ways to keep tension to a minimum. Here are some suggestions:

1) Be vocal.

Tell your parents what's going on in your life. If they feel like you're truthful and open, chances are they will trust you much more than if they believe you're being secretive and hiding your feelings. In that case, they will be more likely to question you and feel suspicious about your social life. You may not want to tell them every detail, but keeping them in the loop about your activities, dreams, struggles and friends will go a long way toward soothing their worries.

2) Be up front about why something is important to you.

If there is something you want to do and you get the annoyingly rigid "no!" tell your parents why the activity means so much to you. If, for example, you're hoping to attend a party on the other side of town so you can see the girl you like, try, "Mom, I'd like to go to this party so I can make a connection with Adrianne. I really like her, and I'd like to invite her to the dance. I will be home by eleven, promise." (If you get the go ahead, just be sure to be home by eleven!)

Rashid, who is 17, understands the importance of explaining his motives to his mother. In fact, he finds it works almost every time.

Rashid: "Mom, I'd really like to go on a fishing trip with Mike and Jake this weekend. I've moved my schedule around so it won't conflict with anything, and I'll only be gone Friday night."

Mom: "I don't know. I'm not sure I'm comfortable with you being out in the woods without any adults."

Rashid: "We'll have a GPS, and the sheriff's office says there is cell phone service at the lake. Mike is very experienced and knows his way around that area. And anyway, I just feel like I should know how to camp and fish. I'm kind of embarrassed that I don't know anything about it . . . especially when my new friends talk about it all the time. This is a good chance for me to learn."

Mom: *"All right. I suppose you should learn how to use a fishing rod. Give me a map of where you're going, and check in when you get there."*

By laying out his motives and plans, Rashid appealed to his mother's emotions and calmed her worries so she felt comfortable supporting his choice.

Parents are just trying to do their job most of the time. They want to keep you safe. But sometimes they go too far, and it's up to you to communicate and explain yourself. Be patient with them, and they'll do the same with you.

POKE → Avoid alienating authority figures and you're likely to thrive in your interactions...and in life.

CHAPTER 11

BUILDING FIREWALLS:
How to say "no" to peer pressure

Saying "no" to a peer can be one of the most difficult things to do, especially when you're trying to be likeable and popular. But caving in to peer pressure and being a doormat in order to have people like you isn't going to elevate your social status or make you happy. Don't let yourself get trapped in difficult situations because you're a pushover.

I remember being a shy teenager and avoiding saying "no" at all costs because it seemed like the best way to avoid confrontations. So I said "yes" to everything from taking on the extra responsibility in a group project to collecting all the balls after soccer practice to spending time with guys in whom I had no interest. But as I matured, I realized that this behavior would only lead people to take advantage of me. It's actually better to learn the skill of saying "no" early on because it's much more difficult to change once people perceive you a certain way.

There are six main steps to saying "no" in a way that prevents you from alienating yourself from your peers:

1) Explain yourself.

People are often under the impression that if you say "no" it's because you're lazy, a prude or uninterested in them. It always helps to elaborate on why you can't do something. If an acquaintance asks you to help her with her lacrosse moves, for example, saying "no" without an explanation is not the same as telling her you can't because you're going to Andy's house to do schoolwork. Similarly, if Gina asks her friend Dana to go to the movies but Dana has already made plans for the night, Dana will be better off telling Gina the truth: "I'm so sorry, but I already made plans with Jenn. I'd love to go with you to the movies tomorrow night, though." An explanation softens the bluntness of the "no" and helps the other person understand that you're interested in him or her, but unavailable at the moment.

2) Don't rush to answer.

If an invitation comes your way that makes you uneasy or unsure, try my favorite response: "Let me get back to you" or another version such as "Let me give that some thought and get back to you." Take some time to examine the source of your discomfort and determine how you really want to respond. At a later time you can text, phone or let that person know face to face that the invitation will not work for you. Let others down sincerely, apologetically and honestly, but never feel pressured to give an immediate response if you don't want to.

3) Be firm.

One of the most challenging parts of saying "no" when you're at such a vulnerable time in your life is doing so firmly. People will press you, so it may take saying it several times decisively and assertively. Some of the most common propositions teens are presented with involve alcohol, drugs and sexual activity. It is often not the "cool thing" to reject partaking in such novel life experiences when your friends are doing it. Here's an example of how to handle such a situation in a nice, yet clear manner:

Martin: *"Hey, Sofia. Isn't this a fun party?"*
Sofia: *"Yeah, I'm having a great time!"*
Martin: *"Can I get you a beer?"*
Sofia: *"No, thanks. I don't drink."*
Martin: *"Why not? What's wrong with you?"*
Sofia: *"I'm just not into it, and I think it tastes disgusting."*
Martin: *"You get used to the taste after you take a few sips. Just try this beer, it tastes better than most."*
Sofia: *"No, really. I'm having plenty of fun without beer."*
Martin: *"All right—you don't like beer. I'll find you a mixed drink, then."*
Sofia: *"Martin, I really value our friendship, so I'd appreciate if you'd stop asking, because I'm not going to do it."*

Martin: "OK, OK."

Sofia did an excellent job of not only holding her ground but consistently asserting her position. In addition, she expressed confidence her friendship with Martin would remain strong if he would pay her the respect she deserves.

4) Try humor.

Using a sense of humor is often an effective tactic if you're concerned about hurting someone's feelings or coming off too strongly. Try these clever "no" statements when you want to use some humor:

> *"No, sorry. I'm on a drug-free diet."*
> *"No, I'm allergic."*
> *"No, it makes me tired and I'd rather be awake for this party."*
> *"Only if it will cure my cold."*
> *"No, but I'll take some bacon."*
> *"No, it kills my game."*
> *"No, I have to be a functioning human being tomorrow."*

And my favorite response to unwanted alcohol, sexual advances or even French fries is: "Thanks, but I'm trying to quit!"

5) Keep the focus on you.

If you keep the focus on yourself so it doesn't seem like you're judging your peer, you can get your point across more effecti-vely. See how Serena tells Nicole that she can't afford to go shopping:

> Nicole: *"Hey, let's go shopping at the mall today!"*
> Serena: *"I wish I could, but I'm totally broke right now."*
> Nicole: *"Oh, don't be lame. You can still afford to buy something."*
> Serena: *"I'm sorry, Nicole, but I really can't right now. I would love to go. I just don't have any money, and I don't want to be tempted."*

Serena expressed respect for their friendship by firmly but politely offering her reason for her unwillingness to go shopping.

6) Provide an alternative.

A helpful way of saying "no" is to offer an alternative. Providing an alternative means you're willing to find a solution for whatever "problem" you might be causing by not accepting what's been presented to you. In the above scenario when Serena is being pressured by Nicole to go shopping, Serena could also offer: *"I get paid for my chores on Sunday, so if you want to wait, I could go to the mall then."* This gives Nicole the opportunity to respond with: *"Fine. I can wait until Sunday."*

In another example, if your teacher asks you to tutor a student a few times a week but you already feel overextended, explain that you have important, pre-existing commitments but could tutor one day a week. Or if a popular football player asks you for a ride home but your parents don't permit you to have a passenger in the car, say you can't but you'd be glad to ask one of your other friends if he or she can. This way, you don't have to use the word "no" at all.

In the following situation, Liam is new to school and has been hanging out with some guys he met in his English class. They were assigned to work on a group project together. Liam is very focused on his grades and wants to make a good first impression at his new school while also appealing to his new pals. See how Liam is sincere, firm and clever about providing an alternative to a troublesome suggestion:

> Brian: "Hey let's ditch English today and go to Liam's place to play Xbox."
> Chris: "I'm in!"
> Eric: "Let's do it! Liam, what do you say?"
> Liam: "That sounds fun, but I don't want to miss anything in class. If we wait until after school, we can work on our project, play some Xbox and raid the pantry. My mom just restocked the snacks."

If he'd just said "no," Liam might not have appeared loyal to his new buddies. If he had said "yes," he would have compromised his dedication to his academics. Avoiding both of these pitfalls, Liam provided an alternative situation to benefit his objectives without completely disagreeing with his friends.

It's important that you decline thoughtfully, with confidence and offer a solution to the issue that has come up. This way, you'll avoid being a pushover and still have the respect of others.

POKE → Know that it's OK to say "no."

SECTION 2

Dealing With Difficult Interactions

CHAPTER 12

DELETING BULLIES FROM YOUR LIFE:
How to quickly rid yourself of troublemakers

Anyone can be the target of a bully, and chances are everyone has been picked on at one time or another. The best way to prevent having a confrontation with a bully is to avoid that person whenever possible. Rather than engage with a bully, report him or her to a trusted adult. A school counselor or a parent is often a good place to start. And if you know someone getting bullied, it is your ethical responsibility to let an authority figure know.

If you're confronted by a verbal bully, be as unresponsive as possible. Don't engage with them verbally or physically, and certainly don't provoke them.

Here's an example of how to get out of a situation in which a bully is attacking you:

Derrick (bully): "Hey Tom. Wow, you're carrying a lot of books. What a nerd. You won't mind if I just knock these out of your hands (laughs). Have fun picking those up."

Tom: "Leave me alone, Derrick, and I'll do the same with you."

Derrick: "Why would I leave you alone? You're so fun to torment."

Tom: "What's it going to take for you to leave me alone?"

Derrick: "What's it going to take for you to try and stop me?"

Tom: "How about I report you? Or I could ignore you, if you ignore me from now on."

Derrick: "Fine, just stay out of my way."

By being calm and persistent about his desire to be left alone, Tom eventually wore Derrick down. Even if Derrick had not given in so easily or taken so well to Tom standing up for himself, he is still much less likely to bother Tom in the future now that he knows Tom won't just quietly take the harassment.

Conversely, being the "mean girl" or "tough guy" at home, school or work will not win you respect, friends or long-term relationships. If you think fighting is fun or picking on people will make you happier or more popular, you've been misled. You need to look inside yourself for the reason you're tempted to pick on others. Bullies are often misunderstood. Although they do and say hurtful things, they're often motivated by underlying fears and insecurities. In order to divert people from seeing that lack of confidence, they prey on others' insecurities.

If something is bothering you, talk to someone you trust—a parent, sibling, teacher, coworker, boss or counselor—to figure out the source of your misdirected aggression. The better you become at communicating, the more likable (and powerful) you'll be.

Survive and Thrive Against Cyber Bullying

What if you're not getting bullied in person, where you can confront the person directly and immediately? What if you're being harassed online? Cyber bullying is a growing issue among teens. In-person peer pressure and bullying may be less common thanks to technology, but digital harassment and pressure to conform can be equally harmful.

The first key to stopping this trend is to avoid being sucked into digital bullying yourself and to discourage others from participating in mean-spirited online activity. From the time you plug in and sign on, keep in mind how you'd act if you were speaking with someone face-to-face. It's tempting to think you're anonymous or safe from confrontation when you're online, but your words matter just as much there as they do in the rest of your life. If you wouldn't do it or say it to someone's face, you shouldn't do it or say it on Facebook (or any other online channel).

This is true even when there's pressure from your peers to participate in bullying online. Just like saying "no" to things you don't want to do in real life, you can say "no" to engaging in certain technology-centered actions, even when they're presented as being "cool." Older generations aren't necessarily familiar with managing online bullying and digital cliques, so it's up to teens to stop internet activity that can quickly become real-life drama, and tragedy.

Here are a few tactics to curb e-bullying evil when your friends pressure you to participate:

1) Positive comments only.

Remember the old adage, "If you have nothing nice to say, say nothing at all"? It remains true, even if you can be anonymous online. If you choose to "pile on" a negative comment to other negative comments you become a member of a gang of bullies.

2) Ditto above.

Don't get sucked into what seems to be the "popular" thing to do. You can avoid getting involved in a situation by saying, "I'd prefer to stay out of this," or by using some of the advice for saying "no" that we went over in Chapter 11. Try diversion: Ideally, by doing this you'll be able to talk others out of acting cruelly. Try, "Guys, we don't need to do this. It's a waste of time. Let's look at the playoff schedule and see if we can get tickets to the next game."

3) Be the leader.

If someone seems like an easy target, find something positive about them. Take the lead on saying something nice and demonstrate that you aren't afraid to show empathy even while others are being mean. Even if this doesn't work, you might earn some respect from those who, like you, don't appreciate the bullying.

What if you're the bull's-eye on a cyber bully's target? Here are some suggestions for how to handle the situation:

1) Recruit help from an adult.

If you or your friend is the target of criticism, tell a teacher, counselor, older sibling or parent so they can help you strategize the best way to deal with the specific situation. You may be embarrassed or unsure how serious the bullying is, but these situations can escalate quickly so it's best to let an adult know early on.

2) Think about ways you can turn the situation around and make it a positive.

Take Stephanie, a fourteen-year-old from Houston, for example. She recently got braces. While no one commented directly to her about her new mouth accessory, she soon became the target of scrutiny with comments made on Facebook as well as pictures of smiles on Tumblr asking: "Did someone lose theirs?" A group was even formed called "Morrison High Metal Mouth," where members made demeaning and hurtful comments about Stephanie.

In Stephanie's case, she turned the negative situation into a positive one by creating her own online group called "Smile for Straight Teeth." With a teacher's assistance, she found other brace-faced teens to join her group and, in the end, had far more members than the group that was formed to tease her.

3) Seek out others.

Find fellow online recipients of negative posts. Take the lead on making friends and posting positive comments to those faced with similar treatment online.

4) Tune it out.

If you can't turn the situation around or get effective outside help, ignore it. Reading (or hearing) things that are negative can be harmful to your psychological and physical health, so turn off the computer or the phone and focus on something else. Find something you like to do to take your mind off it. Don't respond to it, don't spread it to other platforms, and don't try to "get back" at the person—these escalating actions will often just make it worse. Do block the bully from your network (if the site has that option), surround yourself with positive people and activities, and report the harassment to anyone who might help.

Cyber bullying is a persistent problem among today's younger generation. It's up to you to control it. Remember, you don't need to bring people down to lift yourself up. Even when you're behind a computer monitor, that truth remains. And if you're the target do not cave to people who find it easy to sling arrows virtually. They lack courage. Enlist others faced with the same bullying to rally against these cowards. And if all else fails seek out the assistance of a trusted adult.

POKE → If you use your time to create positive experiences and outcomes, bullying can be a thing of the past.

CHAPTER 13

DEFRIENDING "FRIENEMIES":
Eliminating the trauma of false friendships

The notion of "frienemies" (those who pretend to be your friends but are really your enemies) has become a pop culture phenomenon. Although made popular by current celebrities such as Paris Hilton and Nicole Richie, "frienemies" aren't really new. For decades teenagers have struggled with those on-again-off-again friendships that torture them. The whole "can't live with you; can't live without you" thing is a rite of passage for many teens. But that doesn't mean it's healthy. When you develop such a relationship, you must cope with constant ups and downs for it to thrive.

Here are some questions to ask yourself about any friend:

- Does this person support me in the issues and activities that are important to me?

- Is this person happy for me, rather than jealous or competitive, when I experience success?
- Does this person comfort me when I need support?
- Have my confrontations with this person been minimal?
- If I really needed help or guidance, would I call on this person?

If you answered "yes" to these questions, then it sounds like this person is more friend than "frienemy." However, if you found yourself answering "no" more than "yes," you may be in the unfortunate position of having to confront this individual and break ties with him or her, at least temporarily. How do you communicate that you need a break or don't see this person as a suitable friend?

Watch how Bridgette challenges Tara about their rollercoaster friendship without placing blame or being overly aggressive:

Bridgette: "Tara, I feel like we haven't been very good friends to each other, and I think it would be best if we spent some time doing our own thing."

Tara: "Really? I mean every friendship has its ups and downs. You're being kind of dramatic about this."

Bridgette: "I've been thinking this for a while now, especially recently. Our friendship has changed. It just seems we're both busy with other activities.

Tara: "Um, so are we just supposed to ignore each other?"

Bridgette: "I'm saying let's not have hurt feelings if we're busy with other friends. And of course we don't ignore each other, we just have no obligations towards each other."

Tara: "I guess I understand what you're saying."

Bridgette: "Why don't we go about our usual routines and if we see each other, that's fine. But in terms of making plans to hang out, I think we're better off re-evaluating our situation in a few months. If we're meant to be friends in the long run, this is the best way to find out."

Tara: "OK. I guess it's worth a shot."

Take another example. Zach likes hanging out with Kylie, but he feels their friendship is based on superficial things such as the fact that they're both in the school musical and live on the same block. Zach has been having troubles at home and whenever he needs advice or support, Kylie is distant and unhelpful. They frequently argue about the way she treats her friends, and he feels their friendship has been very one-sided. He's wondering if his time might not be better spent with someone who's more empathetic about his troubles, so he makes the decision to talk to her about it.

Zach: "Hey, Kylie, I feel like we should talk."

Kylie: "About what?"

Zach: "About our friendship. I feel like there's a gap between us, even though we have so much in common. I respect your good attitude and think you're very talented, but I don't think we communicate very well."

Kylie: "What do we need to communicate about? We talk all the time."

Zach: "Yeah, but with everything going on in my life right now I think it would be good for me to focus on my other relationships and make some new friends."

Kylie: "I don't understand where you're coming from with this. But if you think it would be better for you I'm not in a position to argue with you. But that doesn't mean we have to stop hanging out, does it?"

Zach: "It's nothing personal, but I do think we should hang out less. We'll still have rehearsals together, but outside of that I think we should spend time with our other friends—it will be good for both of us."

Kylie: "If you don't want to hang out then I'll see you at rehearsal."

Zach: "Thanks for understanding."

At the end of the day, either a person is your friend or they're not. If they say or do mean things, they're not your friend. Of course people make mistakes, and it's always good to forgive those who ask for forgiveness, but if the friendship is like a yo-yo, then it's not really positive or flourishing. It's much better to invest in friendships that are stable, trustworthy and permit open communication.

POKE → Real friends communicate their thoughts and feelings, allow you to be who you are and are there for you in good times and bad.

CHAPTER 14

SELECT THE RIGHT KEYWORDS FOR TEAM PLAY:
Cutting off confrontations by choosing your words carefully

If you've been on a team you know there can be a mix of many personalities in one group. Collaborating on a lab assignment with a partner, working out with a weight-lifting partner, being a member of a speech and debate team or participating on a charity fundraiser can offer many challenges. Different personalities, compounded by stressful situations and jealousy, can create an extremely volatile environment.

The key to working with personalities that don't always get along is to recognize that you're in a professional relationship, not a personal one, and you're working as a team towards a collective goal. If it's best to stay away from a difficult team member, do that, but realize this lack of interaction can impact your effectiveness at the task at hand. Obviously, you can't stay away from your lab partner, but you can take the lead on improving communication. The same goes for a study group member who's not pulling his or her weight. If a colleague is bothering you, notify your supervisor, coach or the adult in charge. You might be able to take on a role that requires less interaction with that person. The important thing to remember is that you're there to do a job and to do it to the best of your abilities.

My friend Kathy's daughter, Nikki, worked part-time at the mall during the holidays. At first she really liked her job, but then one of her co-workers began picking on her and even started antagonizing her in front of customers. Nikki approached her boss and explained she didn't feel comfortable working with the other woman. It turned out Nikki's co-worker was jealous of Nikki's sales record and the fact that she often received praise from their boss. As a result of Nikki communicating with her boss in a professional manner, she received different shifts than her aggressively annoying associate and was able to enjoying doing her job well once again.

Occasionally you might not have an authority figure to turn to when experiencing a difficult situation, and it will be up to you to deal with a conflict alone. Let's say, for example, that your school club has formed a committee to plan a charity fundraiser to benefit a water treatment facility in Kenya. Most of the committee members take their assigned tasks seriously, but Jack doesn't seem to care much about his duties.

He shows up late, jokes with others, and doesn't pay attention to the tasks at hand.

Instead of saying, "You need to..." or "You should...," keep the focus on, "We need to" or "I need to." For example, you can tell Jack: "I need your research so I can complete my part of the project," rather than: "You need to get your research to me." If a member of your debate team is behaving badly towards the moderator, state: "I need us to show the moderator respect, otherwise I'm unable to focus on this debate." Say what you need, not what they need to do, to improve the situation.

Working with people who have different or difficult personalities is something you will deal with your entire life, so it's best to learn how to cope with such people gracefully now. Keep your criticism constructive and focused on "I" statements and most of the time you'll avoid further conflict. Of course, there will always be some people who just don't want to change their behavior or listen to your input. When these people absolutely cannot be avoided, make the best of the situation by taking care of your share of the responsibilities and staying positive.

Communicate the change you want to see in others by setting a good example, seek outside help when you can, and don't let others drag down your own attitude!

POKE → Don't let confrontations impede you from doing your best on a team or in a club or office setting. Use careful conversation techniques to avoid tension.

SECTION 3

Managing The Digital World

CHAPTER 15:

Mastering Two Domains:
Balancing online tools with your offline life

As a teen in today's technology-driven society, it's easy for you to get caught up in the digital rat race. The modern world of text messaging, online chatting, emailing and social networking provides seemingly endless opportunities to connect with other people. And if you're like many other teens, you're probably an expert at multi-tasking with different devices. But with so many platforms for communicating—email, text messaging, Instant Messenger, Gchat, Skype, Instagram, social media, and more—it can be tiring just to keep up with all the various mediums.

We're all guilty of signing up for and onto too many different communication devices. It seems as if there are new outlets every day, so it can be difficult to avoid the buzz and not get pulled in, especially if you feel like you might miss out on something important if you don't participate.

Ariel, a high school junior, says, "It's easy to feel left out of certain jokes or events if you're not participating in all the mediums. Even though it can be a distraction and can be difficult to keep up with, it's better to be part of it than not. Your social life is dependent on and defined by your technology interactions."

As this quote demonstrates, adding more forms of communication can create stress in your life as much as enrich it. The key is to find balance. Simply communicating with friends through *more* platforms doesn't necessarily accelerate or deepen a relationship or bond. In fact, replacing face-to-face interaction with digital dialogue might be doing you a disservice by hindering your ability to actually connect with others on a more profound level.

Look at this example of a distracted conversation through Facebook messaging:

Ethan: "Hi!"
Colin: "Hey."
Ethan: "Check out this video of a cat jumping into boxes <link>.
Colin: "Cool. You going to be in class tomorrow?"
Ethan: "Maybe."
Colin; "Look at this video—this cat jumps in boxes AND baskets <link>."
Ethan: "Ha!"
Collin: "See you tomorrow."
Ethan: "OK."

How much more interesting might that conversation have been had the two run into each other at the park, or met for an activity?

While technological interfaces are important in today's world, don't let it interfere with the power of a 3-D conversation. Instead, learn to control the amount of time you spend with digital communication. This way, you'll open up time for face-to-face interactions that will be more satisfying. Plus you will not be stuck in the rut of shallow conversations.

Here are six steps to effectively manage your technology tools:

1) Focus on quality over quantity.

When it comes to digital outlets for communication, quantity can be an unnecessary distraction. If you focus on quality, it's easier to stop the digital world from dominating your life. Unless it's absolutely essential for your education or family dynamic, I would advise you to limit yourself to four communication methods outside of face-to face interactions. For me, these would be:

1. Cell phone
2. Email
3. LinkedIn
4. Facebook

Others might choose Instant Messenger, Pinterest, texting or Foursquare. It doesn't matter which four. Just choose the ones you find most beneficial to your relationships and try to keep them to that number.

2) Streamline mediums and discard digital disorder.

Take a look at all the methods you use to communicate throughout the day. Are there ways to consolidate mediums? For example, you could aggregate all your instant messages using software programs that allow you to put all your instant messaging communities in one area (I like Trillian). Many applications are available to combine your Twitter and Facebook feeds (TweetDeck is a popular option). When you have fewer user interfaces, it makes it a lot easier to manage your interactions and spend more face-to-face time with friends without having to sacrifice your most precious communication outlets.

You might also consider editing the number of people in your technology network, deleting people you don't really interact with. If you find yourself spending hours at a time keeping up with all the people you follow on Twitter, Instagram, Pinterest or other platforms, then it's probably time to focus on the ones from whom you get real value and delete the others. This might mean going through your cell phone and removing contacts you no longer call or deleting (or hiding) "friends" who really aren't friends on your social networks. This includes people with whom you might be associated because you think they're "popular" or will help social rank. Getting rid of extra names on your Facebook page or in your contact list will help you limit communication chaos.

Also try putting emails in category folders, such as "school," "personal," and "volunteer." By cleaning up communication clutter, you'll simplify your life. This will open up time to actually talk to others face-to-face and improve your ability to be a good conversationalist.

3) Focus on no more than two devices at a time.

When you try to carry on several virtual conversations at once, your ability to focus on each specific one isn't as good as if you were only carrying on one conversation. While it's useful to learn the skill of multi-tasking, it can be unfair to the person to whom you're typing, texting or emailing. Just because you can carry on several conversations at once doesn't mean you should or that your relationships are benefiting from that many interactions. When you can focus on a single conversation, you'll pay better attention to what the other person is saying, offer more to the exchange and better enrich the relationship.

I advise limiting digital conversations to no more than two at a time in order to keep your focus. It might feel uncomfortable at first to not check your phone every few minutes or switch between all your computer applications, but ultimately your conversations will be more meaningful.

4) Limit your time on devices.

It's easy to get sucked into spending hours on social networking sites looking at friends' photos or chatting with long-distance buddies, but limit yourself to a certain amount of time each day, say two hours total. That time could even be broken up to a few periods a day, for example: 7-7:30 a.m., 4-5 p.m. and 8-8:30 p.m. You could also build your technology time into other parts of your daily routine, like reading your emails before dinner every day or checking your Facebook only when you're riding the bus (if you have a web-enabled phone). If you establish a routine and time limits, it will be easier to avoid spending time in the virtual realm that could be better spent hanging out with friends in person, doing homework, working out or engaging in your favorite hobbies.

5) Try to spend as much time talking with your friends in person as you do online or via text.

Instead of Facebook chatting with your friends all night or talking to a classmate about a project on the phone, invite them over to your house. This will make your interaction feel more special, and chances are it will be a lot more fun and productive. You will gain so much by witnessing someone's body language, smile or lack of one. Your smile can make a huge difference as well. Face-to-face is a great way to build rapport with those with whom you wish to become closer. When we're with people, we can better gauge their "temperature": how they feel, what they really think, if a brainstorming session should take a different turn.

Exercise

Attempt to go the whole day without texting on your cell phone or logging into your computer (other than for school or work assignments). What technology experiences were you missing the most? Choose four from the following:

- Texting
- Emailing
- Skyping
- MSN or AOL Messenger or Gchat
- BlackBerry Messenger
- Playing on apps or games
- Facebook
- Tumblr
- Instagram
- Twitter
- Formspring
- Google+
- Other : _____

This should help you narrow down what the most important forms of communication are for you in your daily life.

6) Don't let digital devices take you away from activities you enjoy, such as sports or reading.

It's easy to lose track of time and get somewhat lazy when talking through technology, but don't let that stop you from activities you enjoy! And make a point to divorce yourself from technology when you do these activities. If you decide to go work out, leave your phone at home so you're not distracted by it. If you want to read before bed, put your computer elsewhere so you're not tempted to get on it. It's important to avoid letting technology get in the way of your passions. Catching a meal with friends? Try this fun game: Everyone puts their phone in a pile in the center of the table. First person to touch theirs picks up the entire bill! That should make for good dining conversation.

Communication Overload

According to a 2010 study by Pew Research Center, "text messaging has become the primary way that teens reach their friends, surpassing face-to-face contact, email, instant messaging and voice calling as the go-to daily communication tool for this age group. Daily text messaging among American teens has shot up in the past 18 months, from 38% of teens texting friends daily in February of 2008 to 54% of teens texting daily in September 2009. And it's not just frequency—teens are sending enormous quantities of text messages a day. Half of teens send 50 or more text messages a day, or 1,500 texts a month, and one in three send more than 100 texts a day, or more than 3,000 texts a month. Older teen girls ages 14-17 lead the charge on text messaging, averaging 100 messages a day for the entire cohort. The youngest teen boys are the most resistant to texting, averaging 20 messages per day." http://www.pewinternet.org/Reports/2010/Teens-and-Mobile-Phones.aspx

And a study from Neilson found that individuals talked on cell phones an average of 188 minutes a month in 2010—down about 25% from 2007, due to the increase in text messaging.

http://www.cbsnews.com/8301-500803_162-20023895-500803.html

Shortcuts are not the solution

In addition to dominating much of our modern conversations, technology has created an entirely new way of communicating that combines shorthand, numbers, acronyms and emoticons in a new sub-language often called "text speak." A teen today could practically have an entire conversation speaking in abbreviated code. While that's fine in digital communication, it's inappropriate to use text-speak in face-to-face conversations and more formal scenarios. In fact, you may find that many older adults or those less exposed to digital communication don't understand what you're saying when you use these codes. Although it's quicker and easier to use abbreviations, take the time to spell out words and use proper punctuation when you're communicating digitally with teachers, coworkers, employers and other authority figures. And avoid substituting code for actual words in face-to-face conversations with adults. This will make you look more professional and avoid confusion.

Take a look at the following chart to get some ideas about how best to translate and apply some of the most common technology abbreviations to actual conversation.

Digital Abbreviation	Translation	Real World Application
LOL	Laugh out loud	"That's really funny! You have a great sense of humor."

TTYL	Talk to you later	"Great talking with you today. I'll see you on Monday."
BRB	Be right back	"I'm just going to say 'hi' to someone I've been meaning to talk to, but I'd like to continue this conversation when I get back."
WYGOWM	Will you go out with me	"I would love to take you on a date tomorrow night. Are you free?
IDK	I don't know	"I'm not sure, but I can help you find out."
PTMM	Please tell me more	"That's really interesting; I'd love to hear more."

Remember that even though many older adults understand that younger people use text shorthand all the time, they may still view it as disrespectful or lazy. Make sure you take the time to use proper, formal spelling (and no emoticons) on school assignments, work projects and applications to schools or jobs. The extra effort will demonstrate that you can communicate in a thoughtful, professional manner when needed.

POKE → Cell phone and internet interfaces are bound to be an important part of your life, but finding balance and committing to face-to-face time in every relationship remain keys to unlocking communication success.

CHAPTER 16

REFRESHING YOUR APPROACH TO FACE TIME:
Using digital tools to create in-person connections

We've dissected how to manage your gadgets so they don't eat up all of your time. Now let's look at how to use them to move relationships forward and invite face-to-face communication.

Many in-person scenarios can be intimidating, and the use of technology can assist in making those situations less awkward and uncomfortable.

If, say, you're nervous talking to your crush at school or even on the phone, you can make a connection online first to build a foundation before making that initial in-person leap. Following a person via social media can give you confidence and insight into that special person's life.

After "friending" a person on Facebook, for instance, pay attention not only to what she talks about but the people she follows and the bands or businesses or websites whose pages she "likes." Watch for new photos he posts of himself, his family members and friends and feel free to ask about different shots when you do talk IRL (in real life). When someone posts a photo on a social network, they're signaling that they're open to discussing it. Otherwise, they wouldn't have shared it in the first place.

Let's take a look at Mark and Annie. They attended junior high together and are now in high school. Mark has liked Annie romantically for years, but has never asked her out. They are "friends" on a popular social networking site, and Mark has learned a lot about Annie through that. They leave online messages for each other and note similar interests, including music. Mark has now developed enough confidence to approach Annie at school and engage in a face-to-face conversation.

Mark: "Hey, Annie. How are you?"
Annie: "Great. How are you?"
Mark: "I'm cool. I saw you put up a new picture on Facebook. You look really good."
Annie: "Thanks!"
Mark: "Anyway, I know you really like Rihanna, and I was wondering if you maybe want to go to her concert next month."
Annie: "Sounds awesome. I would love to."

In this case, Mark was able to appeal to Annie's particular interests because he'd made a point of taking note of them while on Facebook. He approached her with a compliment and tuned into her passion for music. By acknowledging a common point of interest, Mark demonstrated that he notices her, knows something about her and shares one of her interests. Mark doesn't sit in a chatroom all day, building digital relationships with strangers, because he knows it's not a good way to establish conversational skills or create a true bond with another person. Rather, he uses his time online to effectively build a network and a foundation for face-to-face relationships.

What if you have an online-only friend and you want to move your relationship with her into "the real world"? You can use what you've learned about the person online to invite her to do something with you and other friends—maybe an event, a concert, or just lunch. Never meet anyone you only know online without bringing an adult or other friends (depending on your age) along, however. Also arrange to meet in a safe, public place. Some people present themselves in one manner online and behave very differently IRL.

In a different type of scenario, it can be helpful to contact someone online if you know you're going to meet them in person soon. For example, Rose's family is hosting a foreign exchange student, Pedro, for a few months. In preparation for his visit, Rose has been exchanging emails with him. She's learned about what he likes to do, what kinds of foods he enjoys and what he hopes to learn while visiting America. And she's shared some of her favorite things with him. This has given them both some security about entering a new and foreign situation and will allow them to quickly grow their friendship.

One warning: Be careful not to pre-judge someone through these types of interactions. A 28-year-old man I know learned via the internet before his freshman year at college that his soon-to-be roommate had starkly opposite political views and musical preferences and came from a completely different family dynamic. He made an immediate judgment that the two of them would never get along. Thankfully they were forced to be roommates, because despite their differences they became and remain best friends. You may learn on Facebook that a fellow student has a passion for a certain TV show you think is lame, but don't make the mistake of dismissing the possibilities for friendship with her without getting to know the person during some face-to-face time.

Another way to connect with others in order to set up face-to-face time is through texting. Texting is a wonderful way to schedule a time and place to meet or an important phone conversation. By texting a request for a good time to connect, you don't have to worry about catching someone at a bad time and not being able to fully discuss whatever's on your mind. Texting or instant messaging, in this case, can be highly efficient tools.

Technology allows you to build relationships, but it only takes you so far. In order to take your relationships to the next level, you must find a way to initiate personal interactions that will allow you to establish meaningful and lasting connections that add real value to your life.

POKE → The internet is great for making friends and getting to know other people, but it's no replacement for in-person connections. Don't be afraid to upgrade your relationships to 3-D!

CHAPTER 17

MAKING ROMANTIC LINKS:
Moving from the digital world to in-person romantic relationships

Romance is tricky. Whether you're 15 or 50, it can be an emotional rollercoaster. As if finding, falling for and maintaining a relationship with the "right" person isn't complicated enough, the addition of technology has merely added to the confusion.

Drew Barrymore's character in the movie *He's Just Not That Into You*, sums it up aptly. When referring to managing a potential relationship, she says: "I had this guy leave me a voicemail at work, so I called him at home, and then he emailed to my BlackBerry, and so I texted to his cell, and now you just have to go around checking all these different portals just to get rejected by seven different technologies. It's exhausting."

While having a digitally-dominated courtship appears benign at first, it can often be detrimental to how you interact IRL. Getting to know someone in person is not the same as falling for someone virtually.

I would advise against a strictly digital relationship and encourage you to communicate with a crush in a manner that keeps face-to-face dialogue going. There are exceptions, of course, but ultimately in-person interaction is the only way to reach a communication intimacy that will propel a relationship forward.

Here are some dos and don'ts when it comes to online "like" and love:

1) Do exchange blog URLs.

Reading someone's blog can expose a very personal side of him/her. Make positive remarks in the comment section to show your interest and to offer thoughts that can be discussed later, when you're face-to-face.

2) Don't Facebook stalk.

Not only is it a waste of time, it will drive you insane if you try to figure out where your crush is, who he's talking to and if he's into you. Instead, do a drive-by on his status updates, or quickly check his Twitter or Instagram feed, and use this to discover conversation points when you're talking with him IRL. Try something like, "Hi, Trey. I saw you linked to a photo from the beach on Saturday. Tell me about the surfing."

3) Do make an effort to send a thoughtful email or Facebook message every once in a while.

For example, if you come across a cool band or great YouTube video, use online messaging to share it with your crush or partner. It lets them know you're thinking of them without replacing 3-D communication.

4) Don't Skype if you don't have to.

If you live far away from your romantic interest, then Skype is a great way to chat about your day. But if you live in the same town as your crush, don't replace in-person encounters with a camera and a keyboard.

There is no need to make relationships more confusing than they already are. Being a teen in "like," love or lust is enough to make even the most sensible person insane, so be careful with your use of online tools when you're in a romantic relationship and remember to still go old-fashioned as well. Ask her to the dance. Invite him to dinner. Hold hands. Be IRL more than HTTP.

And one word of caution: What's put online often stays online. Never put personal information online, break up with someone online, spread rumors or rant online. You never know who'll read what someday, and how a bitter blog post might come back to haunt you.

POKE → With a screen, a Facebook profile or a phone in front of you, you can establish a relationship with a crush, but you won't be connected in a meaningful way until you transfer that relationship to IRL. Without face-to-face time, no IRL relationship will last. Or be all that much fun.

SECTION 4

Putting It All Together

CHAPTER 18

HITTING "SEND":
Putting your new skills to use out in the community

W e've addressed the essentials. Now it's up to you to execute this advice. Get out in the world and try out your new skills. There are so many ways to do this; you just need to capitalize on them!

One of the best ways to break out of your shell and develop stronger communication skills is by getting involved in different activities or organizations in your community. Joining a sports team or after-school club, or taking on a part-time job or volunteer opportunity can be a great way to interact with peers with similar interests and to gain confidence in your conversational abilities. Your experiences will also give you topics and insights to share in conversations down the line.

Take Lauren, for example. Lauren is 16 and not very involved at her school. She has only a few friends because she's focused on her passion for art and spends most of her time outside of class drawing and sketching, particularly fashion designs. Her parents want her to get a part-time job, so she agrees to apply for a retail job at a high-end store where she can gain fashion knowledge.

Prior to her interview, Lauren's mother advises her that rehearsing is essential. She needs to be prepared to answer questions about why she wants this job, what makes her qualified for it, what her long- and short-term goals are and what she can contribute to this job in order to make it a more successful business. She will also need a strong handshake, eye contact and friendly smile, and will have to practice speaking clearly and slowly. In addition, she will want to be prepared to ask questions of the interviewer to show that she has thought about the job and has interest in the company.

Lauren is a little intimidated by all of this at first, so she asks her mother to practice with her. They make a list of questions she might ask or be asked, and they practice going through the entire interview from the moment she shakes hands and smiles to her "thank you" and "goodbye". They run through it a few times until Lauren feels comfortable speaking slowly, clearly and with enthusiasm. Then Lauren asks a new friend of hers, Dawn, to help her out. Practicing with Dawn, who may judge her or laugh, is a little scarier for Lauren, but she does it anyway and finds that Dawn is very supportive and good at asking tough questions.

Lauren goes in to the high-end store confident and practiced, and she nails the job interview! Once hired, Lauren has the job, she can gets to know her co-workers and interact with customers. Being forced to have conversations with strangers and people outside of her typical social circle gives Lauren the practice she needs to have productive discussions in all kinds of situations. It also gives her more things to talk about with others.

Here, for example, we see Lauren talking to her art teacher:

Mrs. Gonzales: "Lauren, the piece you're working on shows a lot of creativity and an interesting linear technique."

Lauren: "Thanks, Mrs. Gonzales. I've been really inspired by my job. The designers send us look books and descriptions of everything, so I'm learning a lot about proportions and construction. My palette is inspired by flowers and gardens, which seem to be a trend right now. I was wondering if I could chat with you later this week about my future in the arts? My new job is giving me some really awesome ideas."

Mrs. Gonzales: "That's great. I'd be happy to sit down with you. Let's plan on Thursday after school."

Lauren: "I would appreciate that so much."

Mrs. Gonzales: "It seems like you're learning some things outside of school and expanding your influences. Keep up the good work and we'll talk more on Thursday!"

Notice how Lauren advanced her conversation with Mrs. Gonzales instead of just accepting a compliment with the one-word answer "Thanks." Because of her job, she is more confident with her speaking skills, has more experiences to refer to in conversation, and feels more equipped to handle interactions with an authority figure. Lauren has also expanded her group of friends and feels much more comfortable relating to both peers and adults.

Jeff, like Lauren, struggled with being introverted and, as a result, isolated himself. When he'd just started his freshman year at college, he didn't know many people at his university. Although Jeff liked his roommate, Tim, he was not as outgoing and often turned down invitations to do things with Tim and his friends.

One day, Tim invited Jeff to accompany him to practice with the school's club baseball team. It didn't require a huge commitment, but Jeff's apprehension about interacting with new individuals made him reluctant to participate. Through some coaxing, Tim convinced Jeff that it would be fun and would not only help him meet people but facilitate a deeper connection to his school. Although Jeff didn't excel at the sport, he took the risk of putting himself in a vulnerable position and hit a social home run by not only participating but spending time off the ball field with his new friends on the team.

Jeff is now one of my good friends and often mentions to me that joining the college club baseball team helped him learn the value of getting involved in activities in order to meet and communicate with others. Today, he participates in various organizations, both professional and social. And his college teammates are still some of his closest friends.

You may not want to be involved with the same people you see every day at school. If so, seek activities in the community that are unaffiliated with your middle school, high school or college. If you don't know what you might be interested in, check events listings on sites like Craigslist and Meetup, or look at community boards in places like recreation centers, libraries and coffee shops. You may be surprised to find out what a great variety of clubs, groups and organizations there is in your community, even if you live in a small town. Places of worship, choirs, dance and theatre groups, foreign language programs and volunteer organizations provide opportunities for you to meet others and play an active role in developing your interpersonal skills with like-minded individuals. When you have something in common with a person—community activism, for example—it makes it much easier to have a dialogue and form the foundation for a lasting friendship.

My friend's daughter, Gina, spent the summer between her junior and senior years in high school volunteering with a synagogue youth group in New Orleans with others her age in a structured program. My friend said Gina returned from the trip with a more gregarious personality and a new ability to connect with others. Although Gina took a risk by participating in an unfamiliar activity, she went in with an open mind and was comforted by the fact that other volunteers in the program shared some of her anxious feelings. She talked to others about where they were from, their families, what types of activities they enjoyed and what their high school was like, among other things. The risk of taking the trip paid off, and Gina came out of the experience with valuable communication skills and life-long friends.

POKE →   Put yourself in a variety of situations to maximize opportunities that can take you from conversations to connections.

CONCLUSION

So, how do you feel? Are you excited to strike up a conversation, ask someone on a date or join a club and meet new friends? Hopefully you'll walk away from this book with the ability to do all these things with confidence and ease.

You've learned that starting conversations can be as easy as saying "Hello" and offering a compliment, and that open-ended questions are the key to moving conversations forward. We looked at the importance of presenting yourself with confident, friendly body language and avoiding missteps such as becoming an interrogator or interrupting. You learned some special techniques for handling bullies and authority figures. We went over some handy tricks for getting out of a conversation gracefully, for saying "no," and for not letting the use of technology interfere with your relationships and personal growth.

Above all, we've emphasized the importance of building good face-to-face conversational skills now so you can approach the world and all your current and potential friendships with confidence and optimism—a skill that will buoy you through your teen years and help you be happy and successful as you move into adulthood. Research has shown that having meaningful friendships is the key to happiness and psychological well-being throughout your life. And it all starts with putting yourself out there and saying "Hello."

I truly believe that in your teen years it's important to force yourself to do things that may be a little uncomfortable. That might mean trying out for a sport you thought you wouldn't excel at or becoming involved in your church's choir even if you aren't the best singer in the world. I promise that if you put yourself in a position to meet others and work on your communication skills, it will benefit you the rest of your life. I hope you will learn to be adventurous and spontaneous when it comes to conversing and communicating. I've found throughout my own life that you never know where a conversation can take you!

_____Also by_____

DEBRA FINE

Feel comfortable in any situation
when you master the art of small talk

www.DebraFine.com

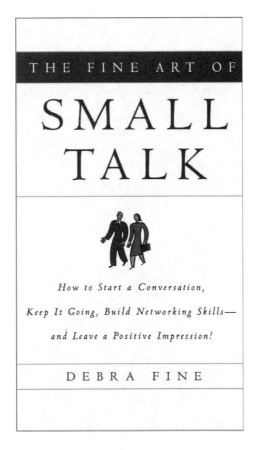